TOGETHER THROUGH LIFE

TOGETHER THROUGH LIFE

My Never Ending Tour
with Bob Dylan

MATTHEW INGATE

Copyright © 2022 Matthew Ingate

The moral right of the author has been asserted.

Apart from any fair dealing for the purposes of research or private study, or criticism or review, as permitted under the Copyright, Designs and Patents Act 1988, this publication may only be reproduced, stored or transmitted, in any form or by any means, with the prior permission in writing of the publishers, or in the case of reprographic reproduction in accordance with the terms of licences issued by the Copyright Licensing Agency. Enquiries concerning reproduction outside those terms should be sent to the publishers.

Matador
Unit E2 Airfield Business Park,
Harrison Road, Market Harborough,
Leicestershire. LE16 7WB
Tel: 0116 2792299
Email: books@troubador.co.uk
Web: www.troubador.co.uk/matador
Twitter: @matadorbooks

ISBN 978 1803130 941

British Library Cataloguing in Publication Data.
A catalogue record for this book is available from the British Library.

Printed and bound in Great Britain by 4edge Limited
Typeset in 11pt Minion Pro by Troubador Publishing Ltd, Leicester, UK

Matador is an imprint of Troubador Publishing Ltd

For my mother,
to whom I owe everything

CONTENTS

	Introduction	ix
1	Chimes of Freedom	1
2	The Blood of the Land	13
3	Shelter From the Storm	25
4	The Streets of Rome	34
5	I Could Have Told You	65
6	Standing in the Doorway	86
7	Clear Through Tennessee	97
8	The Times We've Known	133
9	Can't Go to Paradise No More	153
10	Columbia Recording Artist, Bob Dylan	173
11	Shadow Kingdom	187
	Encore: The Last of the Best	201
	Acknowledgements	227

"I was born very far away from where I was supposed to be and so I'm on my way home"

Bob Dylan, 2005

INTRODUCTION
IS IT ROLLING, BOB?

"**Now** this next one, you're going to laugh at the voice, but ignore that and just listen to the words." My uncle had spent years introducing me to new records and artists – old soul classics released by Stax or Motown, deep cuts recorded at the Fame Studios in Muscle Shoals, Alabama; blues giants like Muddy Waters and mystical performers like Robert Johnson. He introduced me to a lot of beautiful music accompanied by even more beautiful voices, and I already had a taste for Elvis Presley, Frank Sinatra and Carole King before all that thanks to my mum.

I was eleven when he first played me the music of Bob Dylan. When he slipped Bringing It All Back Home from the shelf, put it in the CD player and Subterranean Homesick Blues came blaring out of the speakers, I didn't laugh at the voice. I felt like I'd just been born; that the world was just coming into existence before my very eyes, bursting out of my ears. Colour was filling in everything around me that had previously been black and white.

That year Dylan released Modern Times; his first new album to be introduced to the world since I'd become a fan but the thirty-second studio release overall in a glittering and meandering career.

I first became aware of its forthcoming release when Bob Dylan and Someday Baby featured on an advert for Apple's iPod. Dylan is decked in a rhinestone cowboy shirt in the video and is wielding an acoustic guitar; threatening to send his baby on their way down the road with their clothes in a sack and telling them not to return. I didn't care for the product one bit. I was transfixed by the impossibly old, impossibly cool and otherworldly looking man who had absolutely no resemblance to the Bob Dylan that I knew up until that point.

To return the favour to my uncle for introducing me to Dylan's music, I chose that new album to be his birthday present that year. Again, when we listened to it together for the first time he told me I'd laugh at how Dylan's voice sounded now, and again I didn't find it funny. This new voice was even more beguiling than the first; even richer, more alluring, unique and compelling and brought the world into even sharper focus. Somehow, it was both inscrutable and inviting.

Since that first introduction in 2006, Dylan has released seven more studio albums; with a total of thirty new original compositions and sixty-seven covers. I have seen him perform eighty-one unique songs across twenty-four concerts in eleven different cities around the western world. But before joining up with the Never Ending Tour for the first time in 2011, my travels with Bob Dylan began in New York City as 2007 became 2008.

I'd picked up my own copy of Modern Times in the old Virgin Megastore in Times Square and for the rest of the holiday it never left my Walkman. Whenever I play it now the album transports me back to standing inside Grand Central Terminal and marvelling at the architecture or to being down the line from Hell's Kitchen, where Alicia Keys was born. The old saying goes that the way to get to Carnegie Hall is to practice, but for me it was following the trail that Bob Dylan had left fifty years previously, guided by his aged and ageing voice.

Every subsequent trip to the city, for me, has been an attempt to piece together the puzzle of Bob Dylan's New York; from stopping by the Cafe Wha?, walking down Bleecker Street, Jones, West 4th and MacDougall looking for the ghost of Bob and Suze Rotolo walking arm in arm; sitting on the steps outside his first New York City apartment and culminating with being in the sold-out crowd at Forest Hill Tennis Stadium as he returned to that particular stage for the first time since his first ever all electric gig some fifty-one years previously at the same venue.

Returning by coach to London from the Opal Coast of France in 2008 on another trip, my school-friends asleep around me as we drove through the night so that that same Walkman was my only companion, I spent the time climbing inside another Dylan album.

This time the only disc that span in that old Walkman was Blood on the Tracks. I stayed awake through the whole, long trip listening to the album from start to finish; over and over. Moving from Tangled Up in Blue to Buckets of Rain and then starting the journey all over again.

Each time the album played through felt like I was listening to it for the first time. The world felt a little bit stronger with each listen as the batteries got weaker.

Sometimes when you're travelling with Bob Dylan you don't need to leave the place you happen to be in at any given moment. You can explore myriad worlds through his music and his music can be your guide.

Bob Dylan is the greatest teacher I've ever had. My mother taught me everything I know and he taught me everything else, and more. He has taken me on trips through the ages by slipping references to literature, music, films, poetry, art, history, cultural figures and events into his own lyrics and covered other artists who I have gone on to love as well, whom I likely would never have found without the illumination of his work.

Thanks to him I have listened to Woody and Cisco and Sonny and Leadbelly, too; to the Mississippi Sheiks, Marion Williams and to Charles Aznavour, Helen Forrest and Jimmie Rodgers, Caruso and Gordon Lightfoot. Thanks to Bob Dylan I've listened to Kyu Sakamoto, Edmund Tagoe & Frank Essien and to the Clancy Brothers; to Gene Austin and to Billy "The Kid" Emerson, to Odetta and to Sister Rosetta Tharpe, as well.

Thanks to him I've read Moon Palace and All Quiet on the Western Front, On the Road, Confessions of a Yakuza and Awakening Osiris, I've read Melville, Steinbeck, Dante and Jong; The Odyssey and The Iliad, the Aeneid and Metamorphoses. I've read Timrod and Baudelaire, Rimbaud and Whitman. The work of Bob Dylan contains multitudes.

With Bob Dylan I have marched on Washington, I have been to the grave where the Lone Pilgrim lay, to the Black Horse Tavern on Armageddon Street, bowed down before Jesus, Jupiter and Apollo, have learnt what makes the country grow (it's Anita Ekberg and Bridget Bardot), been on a little street in Singapore, felt a hard rain falling and been lost in that rain down in Juarez (and at Easter Time, too). I've train'd on down to Williams Point and heard that Duquesne Whistle blowing. The summer days and summer nights have come and gone. I've laid down my weary tune, mixed up my confusion and thrown it all away. I've seen better days (but who has not?) and been happy just to be alive underneath the skies of blue. Been Cold Irons Bound, twenty miles out of town and rocked and rolled all the way down to the pit. The world's gone black before my eyes and I've seen my light come shining. I've felt the Caribbean wind and heard the lonesome whistle blow. I've dined with kings and been offered wings. With Bob Dylan, it's hard not to be too impressed.

∞

I saw him live for the first time at the Hammersmith Apollo on November 20, 2011. The day after my 17th birthday and yet again the world shifted, he carries worlds within him and if you're lucky, on any given night he can conjure a whole new one up, just for you.

He doesn't so much as walk onto the stage as appear before you. We queued up all day, surrounded by fellow fans and soon-to-be friends. Standing in the sun of a chill November day for six hours, enjoying an opening set from Mark Knopfler and then suddenly he's there. For the first time in my life, I'm in the same room with Bob Dylan while he launches into Leopard Skin Pillbox Hat. Standing in front of me is 70-year-old Bob Dylan. Wandering outlaw troubadour; pencil tache, bolo tie and all. Standing in front of me is 35-year-old Bob Dylan in white face and flower-decked hat. Standing in front of me is 50-year-old Bob Dylan, down and out and reed-voiced, shabbily dressed and unfocused; a phoenix about to rise from his own ashes. Standing in front of me is 22-year-old Bob Dylan, youthful, smiling and bouncing as he overflows with energy for the music and words that can't stop bursting out of him. Standing in front of me is every Bob Dylan that has been and all those that are yet, somehow, miraculously, still to come.

Being there and witnessing him for the first time, you feel like you're in a room with all of history. Bob Dylan is not a tall man but he is a giant. Like descriptions of Zeus where he is both human sized and mountainous, Bob Dylan is larger than life. I knew by the time the first song came to a close and the lights dimmed that the real journey was just beginning and I needed to be back here with him as much as possible.

∞

I wasn't expecting him to be so lively. True, he doesn't talk much to the audience except to introduce his band (and in later years, not at all). His songs say everything he needs to and more but from the first time I saw him to the twenty-fourth, one of the most alluring parts of a Dylan show is watching how he moves. How he darts and hops and swaggers and stalks across the stage, strikes a flash of a pose and settles back again. A memory of him strutting across the stage; knees half bent and guitar slung over his hip like a gunfighter ready to draw, microphone in his hand while he barked out the lines to Honest With Me on that first night is forever seared into my brain.

The next night we both returned to the Hammersmith Apollo and the magic of being in the room with him was just as electric, just as palpable as he revealed new parts of his catalogue to us, finishing with a duet on Forever Young with Mark Knopfler. And then he's not there, he's gone.

Sometimes I think Bob Dylan is like a ghost, one moment he's there and the next minute he's vanished – slipping back into the night and rolling onto the next show, to the next town, to the next song. He's close enough to touch, he's in the room with you but he's everywhere else at once, too. You ever seen a ghost? No, but you have heard of them.

CHAPTER ONE

CHIMES OF FREEDOM

Wells Fargo Center. Philadelphia, PA. USA
19 November 2012

I'm sitting on an AMTRAK train heading from New York to Trenton, New Jersey. It's the day before my 18th birthday and I've settled in for the ride. I'm staring out the window and watching the city become country and fade back into being city again.

This is going to be the third time I've seen Bob Dylan in concert but the first outside of my hometown of London, and indeed therefore the first time outside of England. Ordinarily, when you're looking forward to a gig the excitement tends to ramp up to fever pitch when you're in the queue outside the venue but as I'm now learning, when you have an eight hour flight and a couple of couple hour train journeys before you even get to stand in line, that excitement builds up even further.

We've spent a few days in New York's Greenwich Village, trawling through the racks of CD and vinyl at Bleecker Bob's;

looking for the Bitter End and sitting underground in the Café Wha?, where the funk band onstage haven't got to pass round a hat to collect their money for the evening's performance like the folksingers who played here in the early sixties did.

But we're not going to be meeting Bob Dylan either in New York or in New Jersey this time. He's not going to be playing in the city that never sleeps until our flights have taken us back to London, so for now we're travelling to him on the huge, silver train; heading from one state to another, and then on again once more providing we make our connection in time.

We're on our way to Philadelphia where tomorrow night Bob Dylan and His Band will be playing the Wells Fargo Center, supported by Mark Knopfler. In my pocket are a pencil and a pad where I have scrawled out my predictions for the next night's setlist.

Part of the magic of seeing Bob Dylan live is in experiencing a moment that only you and those around you get to bear witness to before it's lost to memory, conversation and the wind. Sure, he's going to play All Along the Watchtower and Like a Rolling Stone; sure he'll play Ballad of a Thin Man and Blowin' in the Wind, but will he decide that tonight's the night to dust off You're Gonna Make Me Lonesome When You Go or Jokerman? Probably not. That he might do is exciting in itself – surely none of the 13,000 fans who filed into the Stockholm Globe Arena in 2009 expected to hear the only ever live version of Billy from the 1973 Pat Garrett & Billy the Kid soundtrack album and none of those in attendance at the Recinto Ferial in Spain a year prior expected to be the only crowd to ever hear Bob Dylan perform Handy Dandy from his underrated

1990 album Under the Red Sky, but that's exactly what they got once they'd settled into their seats. On any given night lightning can strike and that's one of the things that keep us coming back to this incredible artist again and again.

We get off the train with plenty of time to kill before the connecting one comes through to take us on to Pennsylvania, so we decide to walk around a while.

Trenton doesn't feel like it should be the capital city of *anywhere*; every house we pass looks like it contains its own unique Amityville horror style story. Three years ago and fifty miles away, a New Jersey resident called the cops on a "suspicious" looking, "eccentric old-man" for peering in through the windows of a house while out walking in the pouring rain. Where I'm walking in Trenton, it's the houses themselves that look suspicious. There's no pouring rain and actually, it feels like there's no weather at all. There are also no people around anywhere I look and it feels like the world has gone grey since we stepped off the train. We're a million miles away from the vibrancy we left behind in New York.

That suspicious-looking man in Long Branch, NJ was of course Bob Dylan. A police officer arrived on the scene and asked for a name and after a short discussion where Dylan could offer neither a fixed address in the area or any personal identification, they ended up giving him a ride in the back seat of their car to where he claimed his tour bus was parked.

Dylan was supposedly looking for the former house of Bruce Springsteen that day in Long Branch. In fact, he was a few blocks away from the house where New Jersey's favourite son had written the songs for Born to Run in the mid-70s.

Around this time, it seemed this was actually a fairly common behaviour for Dylan. In November of 2008, Winnipeg resident John Kiernan and his wife were looking through their kitchen window at two strangers standing on their lawn.

When the doorbell rang, Kiernan opened up and realised the strangers were in fact Bob Dylan and his manager, Jeff Rosen. Dylan asked if this was Neil Young's childhood home, and upon being told that it was he asked if he could come in and see it; to see the view from Young's old bedroom window and to see where he had learned to play the guitar. He asked a lot of thoughtful questions before heading out into the city for more sightseeing and, eventually, to perform a show in town that night.

On a tour stop in Liverpool, England, a year later Dylan visited the John Lennon Museum. After paying the £16 admission fee to walk around Lennon's childhood home, he didn't just stick to the house and even took part in the minibus tour of Lennon landmarks in the city, remaining unrecognised among the other passengers and sightseers all-the-while.

But it goes back further than that, too. Way back to early 1961, when it took Dylan only five days upon arriving in New York for the first time to seek out and visit his then-hero, Woody Guthrie, in hospital.

Into the 1970s, it wasn't un-common to spot Dylan in the audiences of his contemporaries, either, as he went along to watch Elton John, Leon Russell, The Rolling Stones, The

Clash, Bruce Springsteen and even The Lounge Lizards, among others.

Dylan is clearly a fan at heart. Just like those of us who head to cities to watch him and schedule in some stops for sites of particular Dylan interest, he obviously does the same when out on the road.

And it's not just fellow musicians that Dylan is interested in, either. He regularly stops in to the James Joyce Museum in Dublin, Ireland. Imagine unwittingly walking in on the same day and seeing Dylan riding Joyce's bicycle around the room at the instruction of the Museum's curator.

Seemingly intent on *really* giving the singer the star treatment, on one occasion he even instructed Dylan to head out into the streets to take the bike for a real spin.

Other stories through the years include Dylan wandering off from his hotel to walk around Piccadilly and London Zoo unnoticed in 1981 (to the horror of his handlers and to Dylan's delight), visiting Graceland in 1987, attempting to visit Dave Stewart in London in the early 1990s but getting the wrong house and stopping for tea nonetheless with the unwitting homeowner; have him cycling away from soundcheck and weaving his way through the streets of Bratislava, Slovakia before a show in 2010 and pulling his car over on Hollywood Boulevard in 2014 to take selfies with a Spock and a Don King impersonator, even waving a small American flag with the latter (no, seriously) whilst the traffic backed up behind his SUV and most recently, crying in the audience at a Broadway performance of Connor McPherson's Girl From the North Country.

"I've seen pictures of Bob Dylan from a long time ago and he didn't look like Bob Dylan to me at all" said Officer Buble after the incident back in New Jersey, echoing the sentiments of many fans who have left his concerts disappointed over the years at not encountering the Bob Dylan they turned up expecting to see.

This is nothing new – while the number of people who claim not to recognise either the man on stage or the music he's playing has potentially grown as his career has gone on; as his voice has become more battered, used and abused or as his band line up has changed, you only need to listen to the reaction of fans walking out of Dylan concerts in 1966 claiming that he "has changed what he was all together. He's changed from what he was at first", or telling us that it "makes you sick listening to all that rubbish" and – potentially the greatest single line rock review of all time – "Bob Dylan was a bastard in the second half", to know that he has always been an artist operating on his own terms and not on the expectations of others.

Almost fifty years on from that seminal tour with the Hawks / Band amplifying his sound and Bob Dylan is still selling out arenas to fans who turn up to complain that he isn't doing what they expect him to. At the gig I see in Philadelphia there will be no acoustic half to balance out the electric 'set', so any folkies in attendance tonight will think that he's a bastard the whole way through.

Since 2003, Dylan's main instrument of choice on stage has been a keyboard. He has traded in his trusty guitar for the most part to hammer out rhythms on the black and whites. There's no evidence to suggest this is anything other than a creative choice – discussion abounds online about the medical restrictions that stop him from playing guitar onstage anymore, but they seem to ignore the fact that he has both always been a piano player and indeed does still pick up an assortment of guitars in performance from time to time, including on tonight's second song It's All Over Now, Baby Blue.

In his first ever public performance to a crowd, at a talent show at Hibbing High, a young Robert Zimmerman thundered away at the piano so forcefully that he allegedly snapped one of the pedals before having the curtain pulled on him and the rest of his band, The Golden Chords, by the school Principal. That night, Dylan was singing "Rock and Roll is Here to Stay". His headmaster might not have agreed with either the song's sentiment or the way Bobby Zimmerman was saying and playing it, but it's hard to argue when you get to see septuagenarian Bob Dylan hammering the keys as exuberantly as he would have as an aspirational teen a lifetime before on a night like this that he might have just had a point about the genre's longevity.

He's continued to play piano on and off stage for the entirety of his career – whether it's the bouncing beat of Black Crow Blues from Another Side of Bob Dylan in 1964, the obnoxious and goading motif of Ballad of a Thin Man, the tender piano ballads of every version of Spanish is the Loving Tongue, Sign on the Window, She's Your Lover Now or Blind Willie McTell; whether the spirit is moving him through an unexpectedly transcendent version of Disease of Conceit in London in 1990 or whether it's the fierce, driving stabs in 2004 during Lonesome Day Blues that prove the stuff he's got really will blow your brains out, baby

– yet some fans need to take issue with at least one aspect of his show, and recently it's been the keyboard setting he's settled on – a reedy organ sound that sounds like a Calliope setting from everyone's My First Casio Keyboard.

Fortunately and unfortunately, for them – they'll have to find something new to complain about now – this year he has for the most part traded in use of his circus organ keyboard for a baby grand piano and is spending a lot of his gigs perched on a bench to play, surrounded by odds and ends ranging from the Oscar for Best Song he won in 2000 for Things Have Changed to a few bunches of prayer beads. At the foot of his piano a mirror is facing the audience. Whether it's a metaphor for Dylan reflecting their own lives back at them through his art or just a trick to prevent anyone from snapping a decent photograph of him is anyone's guess.

Before we get our first piano song in Philadelphia, though, proceedings kick off with (an organ-led) You Ain't Goin' Nowhere. Immediately, the setlist prediction I made on the train is out the window. We're in a room with 20,000 other people but instantly Bob Dylan has transported us to the basement at Big Pink; the house in Woodstock where this song first escaped his lips in 1967. The first few takes on those recordings – to which the bootleg industry and music fans in general owe a debt of gratitude to Garth Hudson – sound like Dylan is riffing with the language on the spot, somehow not laughing his way through nonsense lines such as those about beating on hammers, heads of lettuce and feeding cats.

Tonight we're treated to a more coherent version featuring references to both Genghis Khan and Roger

McGuinn. The country swing is wonderful and it's clear from the opening number that we're in for a great evening.

It is a wonder that this band and their frontman manage to be so spellbinding, can produce such otherworldly sounding music and arrangements that as well as being transported into the basement of Big Pink I am, gratefully, transported out of the Wells Fargo Center.

It is not a venue that is created with music in mind. It is home to the Philadelphia Flyers in the NHL and the Philadelphia 76ers of the NBA. I almost find it too easy to forget when walking through the forensically bright concourse before the concert begins, surrounded by people queueing to buy hot dogs and popcorn, buckets of chicken and beer that we are about to see a man perform who shared the stage with Dr Martin Luther King, Jr the day he gave his immortal "I Have a Dream" speech; that we're about to see a man who has performed for the Pope and the King of Sweden.

Mark Knopfler kicked off proceedings this evening, as he did last year at the Hammersmith Apollo, moving through a set of songs from his latest album Privateering as well as a smattering of his older solo work. There is a fantastic album on Privateering, if you have the patience to wade through the filler to find it.

His highlights tonight were Privateering's titular track, the rollicking and hilarious I Used to Could, Song for Sonny Liston and the encore, So Far Away.

Knopfler took the stage backed by an enormous Union Flag (as in Great Britain's Union Flag, not that of the United States; although as a major force in the North's Civil War effort one-hundred-and-fifty years ago, we're in a state who would have most likely appreciated the latter) which reminded me of the even more enormous USA flag that Dylan performed in front of in Paris on his 25th birthday in 1966.

Knopfler played eleven songs of his own and quietly returned to the stage once Dylan finished his first track and stuck around for a couple of songs including a ferocious Things Have Changed – complete with fiery ad-libs; after letting us know that the next sixty seconds could feel like an eternity, Dylan roars "and that's a mighty long time!" (with comic emphasis on the "time").

The sounds coming from the stage are muddy, they're swampy and they're bluesy. The band is completely in sync with each other and they are wringing every last ounce of grit from each of the songs they're playing. Dylan is growling and wades his way through Tangled Up in Blue and then Early Roman Kings. I'm a little disappointed that this is the first song from Tempest that I've heard live considering the strength of the other songs on the album, but it keeps on rolling and by the end of the song I've shed my disappointment.

While I'm turning 18 tonight, Bob Dylan turned 71 earlier on in the year. He sounds even older than that; he sounds as old as the whole room of people put together but he moves like he is the most youthful and exuberant person here. While centre stage, vocal mic in one hand and harmonica in the other, he bobs and weaves like a boxer. He nods and dances and floats and bounces with the music, conducting his band with a nod here and a point there, squeezing his hand into a fist to indicate to his drummer, the monumental George Receli, to drive the band into an outro; a stomp of his cowboy boot-clad heel here and a scowl for every imperceptible mistake that only he has noticed, there.

He's singing about rolling, tumbling and crying the whole night long; he's singing about postcards being sold of a hanging and about Abraham sacrificing a son to God on Highway 61 but he's doing it with a smile on his face and a twinkle in his eye so bright that we can see it from all the way at the back of the arena.

Some of my setlist predictions were correct, some would have been if we were seeing him the night before but one of the first things you learn when you get pulled into the world of Bob Dylan is that try as you like, you can't really predict what he's going to do. I would never have predicted that we'd be treated to one of only fifty-six ever live performances of Chimes of Freedom as well as, to date, the final performance of Mississippi.

He's singing for every hung up person in the whole wide universe and he has nothing but affection for all those who've sailed with him. Tonight, I'm glad that I've joined the voyage and set up sail alongside this incredible, unpredictable and spirited artist.

At 18 Robert Zimmerman left home to join Little Richard. Now at that same age, 5,000 miles from my home, I am listening to the siren songs being sung by Bob Dylan. If last year I knew walking out of the Hammersmith Apollo that I needed to see him live again, this year I know I need to travel more often to do so. The Chimes of Freedom are calling me.

CHAPTER TWO
THE BLOOD OF THE LAND

Royal Albert Hall. London, England
November 28, 2013

On July 17th, 2012 Bob Dylan announced his 35th Studio album, Tempest. Shortly after the announcement, we heard a snippet of Early Roman Kings' Hoochie-Coochie Mannish Boy riff in a segment advertising Cinemax's "Strike Back: Vengeance" (me neither) followed by a few verses of Scarlet Town in the show's end credits.

Bob Dylan had played the Hop Farm Festival just down the road from my house on the outskirts of London a month before the announcement was made. My friends and I had decided that that summer we wanted to go to a music festival but when I suggested we go and join 30,000 hippies on a farm in Kent to see the legendary rocker the suggestion was quickly laughed down. We ended up, instead, joining 20,000 ravers on Clapham Common listening to the racket being made by acts such as Knife Party, Skrillex and Benny Benassi.

When I woke up on Monday 27th August, I wasn't sure if the headache I had was a hangover from the night before's alcohol intake or just my brain getting payback for the music it had been subjected to over the weekend. I looked at my phone and saw that Bob Dylan had released a new single. I could hear that Duquesne Whistle blowing through the tinny speakers of my phone and the song's intro, a sepia-tinged parlour shuffle, couldn't have been in more stark contrast to the noise emanating from the giant speakers at SW4.

The drums kicked in and chugged along while Dylan started barking out lyrics claiming he's been accused of being a gambler, of being a pimp but wryly shrugging off that he ain't neither one. One journey on that musical train ride was not enough and over the course of the day, I did whatever the NPR.com streaming link version of wearing out a record through overplaying it is.

When I returned home from school on September 10th later in the year to find my mum had gone to town to pick up a copy of the double vinyl Tempest for me – lauded as a five star instant classic upon release – I practically did wear it out within weeks.

At the Hop Farm Festival, something was happening. A murmur spread online – at expectingrain.com, on Twitter and in the various Dylan Facebook groups – that a baby grand piano had been wheeled onstage before his headline performance. What became more noticeable during this period than Dylan's switch from electric to acoustic piano, however, was the shift in his singing.

Bob Dylan sounded old on 1989's Oh Mercy. He was 48 when that record was released but sounded well beyond those years. It must have been quite a surprise to anyone who had paid attention to Empire Burlesque, Knocked Out Loaded and Down in the Groove where his voice sounded worn out and tired, but he still had the ability to wheeze into his higher register. By the time Oh Mercy came along his now famous rasp was taking shape. Tom Waits started out performing Bob Dylan covers in the early 1970s before becoming an incredible songwriter in his own right, but now it sounded as if Bob Dylan was doing his best Tom Waits impression to return the favour.

Between Oh Mercy and Tempest, Dylan performed around 2,500 concerts. Not much chance for his voice to rest. He stuck with the rocks and gravel approach while singing with the Traveling Wilburys – playfully contrasting his bluesman's growl with the angelic tenor of Roy Orbison; sang with a hybrid of his 80s and 90s voices across Under the Red Sky before seemingly relenting to the age he was wearing on Good As I Been to You and World Gone Wrong.

At times early on in his career he'd sung in a voice that seemed beyond his years – most noticeably on his first record with performances such as In My Time of Dyin' – on which both Dylan and the song sound even older than either really were – or on his haunting live performance of No More Auction Block (Many Thousand Gone) from a concert at The Gaslight in New York in 1962. It is forever a wonder to me how a white 21 year old Jewish kid from the Mid-West can climb inside a song that was originally sung by black soldiers and freed slaves in the time of the American Civil War that deals so directly with the horrors of slavery and sing it with such integrity, feeling and wisdom.

By Oh Mercy he didn't need to *try* to sound old anymore. He wasn't old yet, but he was getting there. The voice suited the songs he was writing for it at the time. It suited the folk and blues covers he released in the 90s shortly afterwards, too, because the songs were aged themselves.

Where his voice really struggled at the time was on stage. Listening to concert recordings from the early 1990s can be a painful task for even a lot of the most ardent Dylan supporters. The issue here wasn't in trying to sound old, but in trying to sound like the younger man who had written the songs that built up his repertoire.

The atmosphere in songs like Most of the Time and Man in the Long Black Coat are leant a gravitas by the gravelly depth of the singer, but on stage when trying to hit a high note or melody written by a man twenty-five years younger, the reediness and nasal whine that is played up in every bad Bob Dylan impression was set to eleven.

Reconnecting with his roots was not just important for Dylan's songwriting, but for his mastery and acceptance of his new voice, too. By going back to the well where he'd first dropped his bucket and pulled up songs like Blowin' in the Wind, Don't Think Twice and Girl From the North Country he could now pull out songs such as Tryin' to Get to Heaven, Cold Irons Bound and Not Dark Yet. Once he'd written a new batch of songs to suit this new road worn voice, he could attack the old ones with more conviction and confidence, as well.

By 2004, what had started out as a growl on Time Out of Mind had become a roar. He's never sounded more apocalyptic than he does in the new millennium. Armed with twelve new songs from the inconceivably good "Love and Theft", Dylan sounds ferocious on the tapes from this period. He sounds like his music is playing as the world around him is ending, falling into itself and going up in flames. His band match him for intensity and they go all the way until the wheels fall off and burn; as the last radio plays and the levee breaks at the last outback at the world's end. Afterwards, he steps off the stage and walks through the flames, steps over the rubble and onto his tour bus and heads on down the road.

When Tempest was released, one of the most noticeable aspects of the album was the voice. The world had had almost twenty five years to get used to the grizzled and gnarly style that has become such a trademark of his latter day work but it seems a lot of people still expect to hear the Dylan of Mr Tambourine Man, of Like a Rolling Stone and of Visions of Johanna. That's not the Bob Dylan who turned up to record at the Groove Masters Studios in early 2012, and he's letting us know it. By the time you get to Pay in Blood, even the four tracks immediately preceding it haven't given you enough warning of the bark that is to come.

※

By the time I next see Dylan at London's Royal Albert Hall, at the end of his 2013 tour schedule, it's like I'm seeing a different man from two years previously at the Hammersmith Apollo or a year ago at the Wells Fargo Center in Philadelphia. He rolled into view in 2011 and 2012 like a gunslinger drifting in to raise hell and take names. He barked out the lyrics and cranked the volume so loud that it's a wonder the roof didn't cave in.

The show that Dylan is now performing has changed a lot in the last twelve months; he is sounding more like an Elder Statesman now than a wolfman stalking the night. The setlist has been revamped and over the course of a spring and summer spent touring North America, his band line-up had a brief re-fresh, too; Duke Robillard momentarily replacing Charlie Sexton until both playing and talking his way out of the band and then Colin Linden holding the fort before Charlie Sexton returned to the fold in July.

The summer tour, named the Americanarama Festival of Music, featured in various places and times opening sets and cameos from Wilco, My Morning Jacket, Dawes, Richard Thompson, Bob Weir, Ryan Bingham, Beck and Peter Wolf. There were surprises in the setlist, too, as Dylan was joined onstage by Jeff Tweedy and Jim James, among others, to sing Twelve Gates to the City, Let Your Light Shine on Me and The Weight; as well as including a cover of Richard Thompson's best song, 1952 Vincent Black Lightning and Bobby Vee's Suzie Baby.

In a spoken intro, Dylan announced that Bobby Vee happened to be in the audience that night and that the singer was the most meaningful person he'd been on-stage with. Dylan is referring to a brief stint in Bobby Vee's band in the late 1950s, when he played piano until Vee let him go; citing insufficient funds to buy Dylan his own piano to tour with. Bobby Vee did later concede, however, that Bobby D could play pretty good piano in the key of C.

At the Royal Albert Hall, Dylan is doing what can only be described as singing.

The volume has come down since the concerts of the last two years with the band playing a more hushed and understated style that allows Dylan the space to sing more softly and not have to bark and holler to be heard. It's most noticeable on songs like Simple Twist of Fate and the heartbreaking, harrowing and gorgeous reading of What Good Am I? where he is singing sweetly and gently, carefully considering his phrasing. The rough edge still makes an appearance here and there, most noticeably on the ominous Beyond Here Lies Nothin' and the biblical High Water (For Charley Patton) but it's not as constant and frightening as in the last two years.

He's added a handful more songs and an intermission to the evening's proceedings since I last saw him and tonight, at least, he's headed onto stage hatless – his curly locks matching the grey embellishments on his trademark riverboat gambler suit.

This venue is grand, the architecture is astonishing and you feel like you're coming out for an evening of high culture. You want to get dressed up for the occasion. Dylan has always had a knack of mixing high and low art – perhaps it's one of the things that makes his work so universal – but this venue has such a grandeur that even later on when he sings about politicians pumping out their piss or tells us that Charlotte's a harlot who dresses in scarlet, it'll feel like an important wisdom is being imparted and we should all be taking note.

Another difference tonight from the Philadelphia show is that the latest record is getting more of an airing.

Last year, the only new song to get a look in was Early Roman Kings and indeed, only a smattering of Tempest songs made their live debuts at all in the year it was released. Now, in November 2013, Early Roman Kings has been joined in the setlist by Duquesne Whistle, Pay in Blood, Scarlet Town, Soon After Midnight and Long and Wasted Years. (Last night Roll On, John was performed for the second and final time.) Of the remaining songs in the setlist, half are from Oh Mercy onwards – one of which is Waiting For You, a beautiful country waltz written for the soundtrack of Callie Khouri's 2002 film Divine Secrets of the Ya-Ya Sisterhood, surprisingly added to the setlist by Dylan this year after only ever previously racking up two live performances, back in 2005 – while there are three songs representing the 60s performed tonight and two from the 70s.

This is possible because of the repertoire Dylan has built up in the second half of his career, writing songs that work with his new voice and his new band. At times, it feels as though Bob Dylan is actually two separate artists, or at least, has had two separate careers. One that spans Bob Dylan to Down in the Groove and another that starts with Oh Mercy and is still pushing forward today.

That the new songs hold up artistically and at times overshadow the tracks from his youth is testament to what an enduring talent and incredible artist Bob Dylan is.

It feels absurd but while his contemporaries and peers seem happy to run out the greatest hits on stadium tours every few years or fade into obscurity or their twilight after a life of heavy living, Bob Dylan seems to get better with age. If you went to see Paul McCartney live and over the course of an evening he played only three Beatles tracks, two from Band on the Run and then decided to focus the rest of his attention to songs from Flaming Pie and Kisses on the Bottom the effect would not be as mesmerising as when Dylan retcons Blonde on Blonde material for songs from Tempest. (Or perhaps, it would be but for entirely different reasons.) The same goes for The Rolling Stones, for The Who and for Eric Clapton or Van Morrison. Bob Dylan is the only artist from his generation who is continuing to consistently release music of at least the standard he set in his twenties.

It is on the stage that Tempest is coming to life. The songs have a much greater looseness, spontaneity and a freedom to them now, compared to on the record.

At its release the songs didn't sound stilted or held back but compared to their live performances, it's hard to go back to the studio versions. It's a good album but hearing Duquesne Whistle, Long and Wasted Years and Pay in Blood with Dylan's clearer voice, more conviction, with a more spontaneous band, a warmer sound and in a live setting has given the songs a new dynamic and has solidified their place among Dylan's oeuvre. I almost wish that he'd go back and re-record the album the way they sound in performance.

A lot of the songs from Tempest were written on the road in 2010, fragments jotted down on hotel notepads from all across Europe. Some of the songs were even tested out in soundcheck on that tour.

While they were finally recorded between January and March of 2012 in Santa Monica, it wasn't until 2013 when the songs became a regular fixture of Dylan's live show that they really started to flourish.

∞

Before the show tonight, my mother and I are walking through the corridors of the Royal Albert Hall getting ready to climb the stairs and take our positions in the balcony. We're looking at the photos of legendary performances at the venue from down the years, including some of a 25 year old Dylan standing on the stage in another lifetime.

As we reach the stairwell we need to head up, we pass by a set of double doors which is for performers' use only. I'm surprised there isn't a crowd surrounding the door hoping to get an early peek at Dylan but maybe his fans know well enough that he's unlikely to be caught walking around where everyone could get at him.

I look up and realise, though, that perhaps hiding in plain sight is a good policy as Tony Garnier, Dylan's long-time bassist, is heading straight towards us and towards the stage door. Pausing to stop for a brief chat, he is gracious and grateful when we express our support and dedication and wish him luck for the evening ahead. After twenty four years on the road with the Never Ending Tour, he must have had a million moments like this with fans but for us, it is more than a nice interaction.

An even more special interaction will come for the fans in the front row later tonight when Bob Dylan steps forward and reaches out to them, shaking hands and bumping fists with a small pocket of supporters all clamouring towards the lip of the stage after he has finished the night's performance with a timeless, fiddle led rendition of Blowin' in the Wind.

∞

Coming back to this venue in two years time, my mother and I will share our own silent acknowledgement with the only man who has been on stage at a Bob Dylan concert more times than Tony Garnier.

∞

Since the late 1980s and early 1990s, the show would begin as the house lights dimmed and a voice called out into the darkness, "Good evening Ladies and Gentlemen. Would you please welcome Columbia recording artist Bob Dylan".

From 1994, that voice and introduction came from stage manager Al Santos, who could be spotted at the side of the stage all dressed in black, goatee grown out long and short hair slicked back.

From 2001, the fourteen word introduction was preceded by a recording of Aaron Copeland's Hoedown and then a year later, following a review by critic Jeff Miers in the Buffalo News on August 9, 2002, the fourteen words became a staggering eighty-eight.

Al Santos could be seen some nights rinsing his mouth with Listerine before picking the mic up, Hoedown dancing away behind him as he spoke, paraphrasing the words from that article that had clearly tickled Dylan so much; "Ladies and gentlemen, please welcome the poet laureate of rock-n-roll. The voice of the promise of the sixties counterculture.

The guy who forced folk into bed with rock; who donned makeup in the seventies and disappeared into a haze of substance abuse. Who emerged to find Jesus. Who was written off as a has-been by the end of the eighties and who has suddenly shifted gears; releasing some of the strongest music of his career beginning in the late nineties. Ladies and gentlemen, Columbia recording artist Bob Dylan."

This year the spoken welcome to the stage has been jettisoned entirely. Perhaps Dylan feels he has reached a point where he needs no introduction.

CHAPTER THREE

SHELTER FROM THE STORM

Trädgårdsföreningen. Gothenburg, Sweden.
July 15, 2014

I'm sitting on the bank of a river in Gothenburg listening to Bob Dylan's band run through their soundcheck on the other side of the water, where a huge stage has gone up overnight in the Trädgårdsföreningen. I had heard a faint hint of music in the air through the window of my hotel room and grabbed my keys and coat and walked the short distance to a spot right behind where the stage was set. Most prominent of all the sounds I can hear is Donnie Herron's pedal steel guitar, wailing into the expansive park.

One of my favourite parts of Dylan gigs is watching the interplay between him and his band, and he seems to have a special connection with Donnie Herron. Occasionally they'll share a joke and a laugh with each other and at other times they'll both spontaneously and simultaneously lock into a riff together and pull the rest of the band along with them to see where it goes.

Another one of the great draws of seeing Dylan perform live is the opportunity it affords to travel. He tours so relentlessly that you have an excuse to get away and see the world most every year. I decided on this date in 2014 because Sweden is a beautiful country and because the cost of flights here from the UK is so absurdly cheap.

※

It's been seven years since I first came to this country; falling in love with the people and the culture. The air feels fresh here, and there is a freshness abound in general. London, where I live, is smoggy and muggy; in Philadelphia the air was heavy and oppressive and on a non-Dylan related trip to Lille last year, whatever fresh air there was was undermined by the sun heating up the contents of the city's open sewer systems; none of those things are a problem here in Sweden.

Gothenburg is stunning. It's not a huge city but there's a lot to see if you take the time to look. Like London it's a city of variety; you may find yourself walking down one street that's paved with cobbles and lined with small brickwork houses before turning onto a street with buildings of concrete and glass growing high out of the ground. There's revelry and a warmth here that bubbles over from a lot of the outdoor seating areas of cafés and bars.

The last time I came to Sweden it was so cold that when the fountains froze over in the city centre of Stockholm, opportunistic locals arrived on the scene to rent out pairs of skating boots. At twelve years old I was young enough not to be scared of trying to skate for the first time there on the frozen fountain. This time, in Gothenburg, it's the middle of July and the slight sunburn I've managed to develop tells me there's not much likelihood of repeating that particular activity.

The country has a rich history of folklore and when you're in Stockholm, most every shop you go into sells a plethora of miniature troll statues – some adorned with Viking style helmets, some donning shields draped in the Swedish flag, some with comically large noses or eyes. Here in Gothenburg it seems the local mascot is not the mythical troll, but one of nature's most majestic creatures, the moose.

It seems that despite the city's trinket shop obsession with the wonderful creatures – it's hard to go into any shop without finding at least a tea-towel, ashtray or keyring featuring a cartoon moose – actually being able to encounter one of Europe's largest land mammals in the wild will be out of the question, as they prefer the ranging woodland and cover of the forest outside the major cities. Luckily for them, Sweden has no shortage of dense woodland.

I'm staying in Gothenburg's oldest hotel – the Hotel Royal – which is a beautiful building that dates back to the 1850s and is only a stone's throw away from where I will see my first open air Bob Dylan concert. The room is finely decorated but tiny and that's not going to be a problem; I'm here to see the city and to hear the music, not sprawl out in a fancy hotel room and miss out on what's going on outside the two hundred year old brickwork.

There is something for everyone in the city, whether you want to head to the stunning Göteborgs stadsmuseum (Gothenburg City Museum) in the domkyrkodistrikt (cathedral district), the konstmuseum (Museum of fine art) or, like me, head up to the Universeum; where you can wander with childlike wonder through a tropical rainforest, planetarium and eventually make your way up to the roof where there are surprisingly life-like, and life sized, animatronic dinosaurs (complete with feathers, a feature that is both scientifically accurate and more realistically done than in other similar installations that I have seen elsewhere before).

If you catch the tram and head out of the city centre, there are some wonderful record shops to lose both yourself and a fair few kronor in, as indeed I have, and it's only when I get back to the hotel that I wonder how I'm going to fit my new stash of Dean Martin, Johnny Cash and Tom Waits treasures into the tiny bag I've brought along with me.

Back in the busier streets of the city centre there is a kiosk that looks like it should be the entrance to a disused underground metro station but which turns out to sell the best vegan hot dogs I've had anywhere in the world.

Before heading to join the queue outside the Trädgårdsföreningen, I make one final tourist stop – the Olhallen 7 an – Gothenburg's oldest pub, taking the three steps down into a bar that somehow feels simultaneously ancient and contemporarily hip. It turns out I have walked into the Bob Dylan of Gothenburg bars.

∞

Up until now, it's been a clear day but the sky has filled with clouds as the line of concertgoers grows behind me. A busker is making his way from the front to the back and to the front again while playing It Ain't Me, Babe. I wonder if he just likes the song or is wryly acknowledging that he really isn't the one we're looking for. I'm here to hear the songs, but more importantly to see *the* man who sings them.

As a previously unannounced Swedish performer takes to the stage to open the night's festivities the heavens have opened, holding out for his whole forty-five minute set and only clearing up and drying off as Stu Kimball struts onto the stage rocking a riff on his strat and Bob Dylan and the rest of his band follow suit behind shortly.

In Philadelphia the setlist blew me away and a year later in London his voice did the same, tonight the two will combine for an unbelievable and unforgettable night.

The band kicks in alongside Kimball and after a few bluesy bars, the crowd get ready to sing along with either Leopard Skin Pillbox Hat or Rainy Day Women #12 and #35 – *surely* that's what this riff is gearing up to be? – "What's the matter with me, I don't have much to say…" Dylan croons. They're opening with Watching the River Flow, a nice touch considering our proximity to the Göta älv river running through the city and the exact activity I was unconsciously engaged in while listening to the sound check earlier in the day. He's playing the piano like he's been possessed by Little Richard and his voice is clear and powerful.

We're one song down and this is already the best I've heard Dylan singing in person. His phrasing is impeccable – indeed his phrasing and conviction are two of the key components that have made him one of the most important, vital and influential singers of the twentieth and twenty-first centuries – and the band are locked in tight. Far from doing his best Tom Waits impression or singing through his nose with arrangements he no longer has the range for, tonight's version of Bob Dylan sounds just like an aged version of the singer who fronted 1975's Rolling Thunder Revue.

Before the applause can die down, they have launched into a jaunty country version of Don't Think Twice, It's Alright. For such a heart-breaking song, this band really does make it swing and Bobby takes a mesmerising, scorching piano solo at the end before they finish things off with a swaggering blues turnaround.

The opening riff of the next song leaves no room for mistaking what it is and we're treated to Just Like Tom Thumbs Blues. By the time To Ramona comes and goes, I feel like I'm going to be treated to a concert where Dylan plays exclusively songs I've not heard him perform in any of the previous three years. He leaves the 60s for the first time tonight with song five, potentially referring to the river behind the stage again – this time more forebodingly – with The Levee's Gonna Break.

So far tonight, every note has been perfect, every line delivered in the way that it should be delivered right now and every arrangement has been incredible, the crowd is held in rapt attention as we are delivered a masterclass in handling a legendary catalogue such as Bob Dylan's. Anyone who says he can no longer perform or sing needs only listen to the inevitable bootlegs that will be made of this show and uploaded to expectingrain.com as soon as the concert is over.

It's already been an incredible show but as it rolls along, it's clear that we ain't seen nothing yet. Moving from "if it keeps on raining the levee's gonna break" at the piano to "come in, I'll give you shelter from the storm" at centre stage

– an opening strum of Stu Kimball's acoustic guitar and a slight grizzle that is the hangover from the bark-singing years and Dylan begins to croon from the second verse onwards with a smoothness and warmth to his voice not heard since Nashville Skyline in 1969. It is a mesmerising performance and a rarity of a song I wasn't expecting to ever hear live.

When I first heard Bob Dylan singing in concert, despite the power; despite the confidence, conviction and the menace in his voice, I never expected to hear him sing this sweetly, this gently. That he would go one better and drop the gravel entirely only two songs later for as beautiful, tender and moving a rendition of Girl From the North Country as I've ever yet heard is incredible.

Of the seventeen songs that have been performed tonight, ten of them are tracks that I haven't heard them play before over the last three years, including all those mentioned above as well as A Hard Rain's A-Gonna Fall and Lonesome Day Blues. Only two of the songs he sings for us featured in his setlist from last night's gig at the Sofiero Palace in Helsingborg, Sweden. I wonder how with a back catalogue of over 600 songs to choose from Dylan can ever possibly narrow down the tracks he'd like to play on any given night to just twenty or so; but as the last song echoes around the park, as Bob Dylan and His Band line up centre stage to stare us down and soak in the applause and as the crowd turns and disperses back into Gothenburg, I'm grateful that however he decided, these were the songs he settled on for tonight.

On the first night in Hammersmith, my grandad remarked to me walking out of the venue that his voice sounded more like percussion than singing. Tonight under the darkening sky in the Swedish summer, Bob Dylan is singing as well as he ever has.

Even on the faster, rockier or bluesier songs, that percussive bark is being phased out. There are times where he leans into it for effect, but the speed at which he switches back to the clear and clean tone that makes up most of the night's performance shows that it is more an artistic choice than a worn down and weathered voice.

He is reinventing himself for us, yet again. At 73, there are new Bob Dylans yet to come, yet to be dreamed up and born. Of course there are.

∞

Later in the year on November 23rd, Dylan performed a concert for one man, the Swedish presenter Fredrik Wikingsson.

The unique concert, performed and recorded at the gorgeous Academy of Music in Philadelphia, PA was part of the "Experiment Ensam" (Experiment Alone) television show in Sweden, in which Wikingsson takes part in events and situations alone in which you would normally be in a group or a crowd, to see how the experience differs.

Dylan performed four covers for him – Buddy Holly's Heartbeat, Blueberry Hill (in a totally unique, minor key lament version), You're Too Late by Lefty Frizzell (and previously only played in public by Dylan once in 1999) and the blues standard Keys to the Highway – before engaging in a light-hearted chat with the presenter and strolling off stage.

That day in November Dylan was performing to just one audience member. Back in July, he made the expansive open air Trädgårdsföreningen feel so intimate that it felt like he was singing just for me.

CHAPTER FOUR

THE STREETS OF ROME

Terme di Caracalla. Rome, Italy. June 29, 2015
Royal Albert Hall. London, England – October 21, 2015
Royal Albert Hall. London, England – October 22, 2015
Royal Albert Hall. London, England – October 23, 2015
Royal Albert Hall. London, England – October 24, 2015
Royal Albert Hall. London, England – October 25, 2015
O2 Guildhall. Southampton, England – October 30, 215

Bob Dylan has spent his life on stage. Since his return to touring in 1974 after an eight year hiatus he has given at least one public performance in every year except 1977 and 2020 – and even in the latter, it took a pandemic to keep him off the road. He has answered the calling to perform with a relentless energy and fervour; joining a tradition of musicians who live by, and on, the road.

Whether it was the surprise four hour concert at Toad's Place in New Haven, CT in 1990 or the Rolling Thunder Revue; the night in the early 1980s when he picked up a saxophone on stage and blew, or any of the countless occasions he has performed a song in concert for the one and only time, he has repeatedly shown what an unpredictable artist and performer he is.

When he took to the stage on February 6, 2015, to receive the MusiCares Person of the Year award – presented to him by long-term friend President Jimmy Carter – he gave a performance that was perhaps more surprising than any other in his long and unpredictable career.

He didn't pick up a guitar or sit at the piano; didn't sing or blow into a harmonica. Instead, he spoke. And at length. Apparently Bob Dylan doesn't talk when he's on stage but leaning against the podium at the Los Angeles Convention Centre, he spoke for around 35 minutes, meandering from one thought to the next to a captivated room.

"Why me, Lord?" He asked after pulling up the critics who claim he can't sing; suggesting that he gets preferential treatment and that those same critics should take a listen to Tom Waits, Lou Reed or Leonard Cohen.

If the thirty-five minute acceptance speech was surprising, the release of Shadows in the Night shortly before was astounding. Ten "Frank Sinatra Covers" (never mind that only one of the songs was even co-written by Sinatra and that they've all been recorded and sung by everyone from Billie Holiday to Seth MacFarlane) transposed from 30-piece orchestra recordings to late night whiskey bar hymns by Dylan and his five piece band, the album is a triumph in performance and in wringing out emotion from lyrics that a lot of other performers miss entirely when they sing them and served as yet more proof that those critics who claim he can't sing should try listening to him once in a while.

Dylan does have a special connection with Sinatra, though. He regularly played his songs on Theme Time Radio Hour and has spoken warmly about him across plenty of interviews. At a party to celebrate Sinatra's 80th birthday, the legendary crooner pulled Dylan to one side and told him, "You and me, pal, we got blue eyes, we're from up there", and he pointed to the stars. "These other bums are from down here".

Dylan first performed That Lucky Old Sun to a live audience at Farm Aid in 1985. It became a semi-regular inclusion on the following year's tour with Tom Petty & The Heartbreakers, but thirty years later on Shadows in the Night, it is a whole new song – completely inhabited and owned by Dylan and a triumphant conclusion to what is a stunningly good album.

The singing is whiskey soaked and cigar aged, the performances hushed, understated and entirely appropriate to the mood of the record. It's perfect late night listening. Gone is the grizzle and gravel of Tempest and Together Through Life, banished is the bark and wolfman growl of the 2011 tour or the fiery apocalypse of his 2004 voice. This is an album where Dylan sings sweetly, reminiscently and fondly, just like he did when I saw him sing Girl From the North Country and Shelter from the Storm last year in Gothenburg.

These are most likely songs that would have played in the Zimmerman household where young Bobby was growing up; floating in the air on the radio while his mother Beatty was cooking in the kitchen and must have a sentimental value for Dylan that we can only guess at, but it might explain that reminiscent tone that is creeping into his voice as he approaches the September of his years.

Back on stage at MusiCares, he gave thanks to those songwriters and performers who appreciated, championed and helped him in his early days – Doc Pomus, Johnny Cash, Jimi Hendrix, Joan Baez, Sam Philips, Pervis Staples, Nina Simone – and revealed the secret of his songwriting: absorbing what came before him.

He reeled off lyrics to folk songs he'd performed countless times as a young man and how that effected the words he went on to write. Anyone who was surprised by this has not been paying attention.

His own lyrics have always been peppered with references, allusions and downright appropriation to and from the songs that went before him; whether it was the melody to Blowin' in the Wind (No More Auction Block), Sugar Baby (The Lonesome Road), Don't Think Twice It's Alright (Who's Gonna Buy You Ribbons When I'm Gone?) or Tweedle Dee & Tweedle Dum (Uncle John's Bongos) or taking a phrase here and there from movies, books, folk songs, poetry or plays; creating something new from something old has always been a part of Dylan's alchemical process. Steal a little and they throw you in jail, steal a lot and they make you king.

Where Shadows in the Night stands up so well is that he is making something brand new out of parts he hasn't put together himself. He's making these old songs sound fresh – "un-covering" them, as he put it in one promotional interview for the album. The recording somehow sounds vibrant and immediate, but also like it has existed forever already. That the album *sounds* as good as it does is in part down to the legendary producer recruited to oversee recordings, Al Schmitt.

Schmitt had worked on these songs before, on the Sinatra Duet albums in the early 1990s, as well as with Ray Charles on his Genius Loves Company record. He was one of the warmest, most sincere and talented individuals the music industry has ever seen.

Covers have always been a big part of Dylan's performance; whether it was singing folk songs in his formative years, rock and roll classics all through the 1980s or singing songs written by his contemporaries like Gordon Lightfoot, Johnny Cash or John Prine; he seems to look backwards to look forward and move his own artwork on after a period of absorbing what went before him.

After the early folk years came The Freewheelin' Bob Dylan and The Times They Are A-Changin'; after Self Portrait and all the covers recorded in the Big Pink basement with The Band or at the sessions in Nashville around 1969 and 1970 came Blood on the Tracks and Desire, after World Gone Wrong came Time Out of Mind and "Love and Theft". It's exciting to have Shadows in the Night in and of itself, but it's also exciting to wonder what he will come up with next, now that he seems to be going back to the creative wellspring, again.

∽

Another source of inspiration for Dylan, it seems, is a much older form of folk song.

The epic poetry of Homer was originally passed down

through performances and word of mouth – the events of the Iliad and the Odyssey taking place around the 13th Century BCE and written down for the first time in the 8th Century BCE before being lost in the Middle Ages and making a comeback during the Italian Renaissance period.

Dylan seems to have a particular fascination with the classics and ancient texts; whether it's references to Dante in Tangled Up in Blue ("written by an Italian poet in the 13th Century") or directly being inspired by phrases from Ovid ("I'm in the last outback, at the world's end"), Homer ("Would to god I could strip you of life and breath and ship you down to the House of Death"), or from Virgil ("to teach the ways of peace to those you conquer, to spare defeated peoples and tame the proud") among others.

It was a character briefly mentioned in Homer's Iliad and immortalised in Virgil's Aeneid, Aeneas, who escaped the Battle of Troy and made it to Italy – mirroring the scrapes of Odysseus in the Odyssey by skirting past Scylla and Charybdis, landing on the island of the Cyclopes and descending into the Underworld – before going on to become the ancestor of the Romans, and therefore, the grandfather of the city that I will next see Bob Dylan in.

∽

Rome is a city of marvels and it is a city of Gods, old and new. It's a city where all time comes together and history is in the air. You can feel it in your lungs as you walk the streets of Rome; outside the Colosseum and beside the Trevi Fountain, peering up at the Pyramid of Cestius, swinging by the Spanish Steps or praying at the Pantheon.

I've paid to join a guided tour of the Vatican, avoiding the queue which will apparently take three hours to work through. Whether this is true or a tactic the ticket seller for the tour uses to hasten up a sale, I don't know but as we walk past the hundreds of people waiting to get in and through the gates, I don't mind one bit.

Stepping into the Vatican City is like stepping into the past; stepping hundreds of years back in time. It is the smallest independent state in the world in terms of both size and population, yet it has one of the biggest influences and impacts on Western culture and history.

The Vatican Museums are home to the most incredible array of artefacts: paintings from the middle ages to the 19th Century including masterpieces by Giotto, Leonardo da Vinci, Raphael, Perugino and Caravaggio; statues in the Pio Clementino Museum presenting scenes and legends from Ancient Greece such as the Laocoön sculpture group and Perseus with the head of Medusa and of course, Michelangelo's Sistine Chapel.

Walking through the sheer weight of the history that is housed here, I am struck by the sheer amount of gift shops and souvenir stands all throughout the grounds. It feels like that for every hallway you pass through housing an ancient masterpiece, you have to pass through a gift shop on the way in and the way out. It's easy to see without looking too far that not much is really sacred, indeed.

Outside, the sun is scorching everything here and as well as the weight of history, there is an oppressive heat in the air. The day before I arrived at Rome's Fiumicino airport a fire broke out in the underground baggage area at Terminal

3. When I landed, half of the airport was closed off and it felt like walking through a wasteland. Passengers around me complained that EasyJet is far from an easy airline to fly with. I am impressed we weren't rerouted or delayed further.

Back home, London is experiencing a heatwave. On my way to the airport the Gatwick Express was delayed due to fears that the heatwave was rendering the train tracks dangerous. The 31°C heat in London was surely lower than that of the flames that worked their way through the Italian airport. Already I was sensing that people here are more resilient than they are back home.

I am sat outside the café I have been to every morning since I arrived. After I struggled to order what I was aiming for on the first day, the barista has kindly learnt what I was really after and starts preparing it each time I step inside.

I'm in the shade reading On the Road. On the back is a quote by Bob Dylan confessing that the book "changed my life, the way it changed everyone else's". Perhaps I should have packed some more appropriate reading material considering the location, Dante or Virgil, but On the Road at least still feels relevant enough with its sense of freedom, movement and electricity; all the things I'm chasing whenever I follow the path set out by Dylan and his band. It is the third time I have read it.

∞

This evening in Roma, I will watch Bob Dylan and His Band at the Terme di Caracalla. Ever since the date was announced and I saw a photo of the incredible venue, I knew that this was where I wanted to see him.

The venue is what is left of the second largest thermae, or, public baths of ancient Rome. During the day you are free to wander the grounds and get lost in the labyrinthine sprawl of crumbling brick; the ruins rising out of the ground as if they are part of the earth itself and as if they have always been there. Perhaps they always have.

There are a few people around but I take a left turn and enter out into a courtyard. The stone path has become grass, here, and I'm enclosed by the towering ruins. The sun is shining in through an arch and casting shadows on the ground, a place to stand to get a momentary respite from the heat.

There is no one else in this courtyard, no other tourists or locals have gotten lost in the maze quite the same way that I have, or at quite the same time. I think about how much busier this site would have been in 212 AD when it was first opened, staying busy and staying open until being abandoned 350 years later.

What did the people who came here talk about? What kind of lives did they lead? What did the structures look like when they weren't falling apart at the seams?

Since the late 1930s the Terme di Caracalla has been the home of the Rome Opera company. On the day I return to London, the summer opera season is due to kick off here with a production of Madama Butterfly. With better planning I would have delayed my journey home to be in attendance.

Never mind. I'm still going to be here tonight at least to witness Bob Dylan perform in front of the imperious scenery, so I make my way back out of the labyrinth – without the guidance of Ariadne's thread – and head back up to the main entrance, taking my place in line, ticket clutched tightly in my hand.

∞

My excitement for the show started building to fever pitch on the 19th May as I stayed awake until the wee small hours to watch Dylan's performance on David Letterman's penultimate show as host of his long running Late Night programme.

It was the fourth performance he'd given on the programme and his fifth appearance overall. The first, on March 22nd, 1984 is classic Dylan.

Appearing on the programme to promote his then-latest record, Infidels, Dylan was backed by a band of young LA musicians called The Plugz. They'd been jamming together at Dylan's Malibu home and transformed his sound entirely.

What on record had been a reggae and middle of the road rock infusion became urgent, insistent and driving punk on stage; kicked on by the young band he was performing with and the spark they'd lit under Dylan. On the show, he had the sleeves of his pencil thin suit rolled up and his tie hanging loose. He was clearly ready for business.

Dylan leads the band through three songs and is as energetic and full of fire as you will ever see him, dropping down to his knees and bouncing back up and prowling the stage looking for a harmonica in the key he needs, leaving his band to roll on alone while he wanders confidently and nonchalantly off screen.

After the show he was sat in his dressing room when Paul Shaffer, Letterman's long-time band leader, stuck his head around the door and tried to engage the singer.

"You know, Bob," he said, "you grew up just 130 miles to the south of my hometown in Canada. We're linked by Highway 61. And I've got to tell you something else. Just like you I spent my growing-up years with my ear pressed against a transistor listening to those faraway southern radio stations. Just like you, I learned to love rhythm and blues. And hey, Bob, how about that Bobby Vee? You played piano with him. I could sing both parts to 'Take Good Care of My Baby.' We're soul brothers! When you sang Roy Head's 'Treat Her Right' in rehearsal today, Bob, it sounded just great. I wish you'd record it." Presumably pausing to take a breath after such a long opening monologue, Shaffer finally allowed Dylan the space to respond.

"Hey Paul, think you could introduce me to Larry "Bud" Melman?" was all he said.

He didn't return to Late Night to perform until the show's ten year anniversary in 1992 when he was backed by an all-star band including Carole King, Steve Vai, Chrissie Hynde, Mavis Staples, Rosanne Cash and Emmylou Harris for a ramshackle yet endearing version of Like a Rolling Stone.

A year later Dylan was back on the late night stage to sing a stripped back Forever Young, looking much more relaxed and comfortable surrounded by his own backing band.

In 2015 he sent Letterman off with a stunning reading of The Night We Called it a Day, a fitting goodbye to one of Late Night television's most iconic hosts.

Tonight in Rome the band stroll onstage right on time, calmly and in no hurry. Dylan is close behind, peering up at the huge structure behind him; the ruins towering overhead. He heads straight for his piano without looking out over the crowd and joins in as the band have already launched into Things Have Changed.

During the third song he references the ancient Roman poet Ovid ("beyond here lies nothing but chillness, hostility, frozen waves of an ice-hard sea") who was exiled from this land almost two thousand years ago.

In the next song there are scores of Ovid references but what is even more startling is the completely rewritten lyrics to Workingman's Blues #2. I'm sat on the edge of my seat, trying to lean into the sparse and haunting music as much as I can to take in each new wonderful image.

No longer is Dylan singing about being tossed by the winds and the seas and bragging of dragging those who've wronged him to hell and selling them out to their enemies, now he is leaving everything behind and fretting about being robbed by bandits.

The place is no longer ringed with countless foes who may or may not be deaf or dumb; now Dylan is waking up in the morning, leaping to his feet and heading into town, on a whim. He sees his father in the street, or, at least he thinks that it's him.

Before he found no blame in his companion and told them that "no one would ever claim that I took up arms against you" (directly quoting Ovid) but now he is wrathful and is warning that "I'll punch my spear right straight through / half-ways down your spine" (now directly quoting Homer).

At the end of all this, he looks around and asks, "Look at me, with all my spoils / what did I ever win?" before building up to one final chorus and the song is gone. I felt like I dreamed all the new words and wish they'd play it again right straight through so I could take them all in properly.

Throughout his career Dylan has tinkered with his songs on stage, whether it's new arrangements or new lyrics, most famously with Tangled Up in Blue in 1978 and 1984, If You See Her Say Hello in 1976 and 2002 or all the versions of Tonight I'll Be Staying Here With You, I'll Be Your Baby Tonight, Knockin' on Heaven's Door, Gotta Serve Somebody or Simple Twist of Fate through the years but this reworking is particularly astounding. So little of the original song remains, melody or lyric, that he has made something new out of something old, even within his own repertoire.

The night is closing in as the music rolls on; the sun is falling behind the largest of the ruins at the farthest perimeter of the stage and the moon is clearing its way through the clouds just in time for Dylan to launch into Full Moon and Empty Arms. It is a delight and his voice sounds even sweeter and more sincere than on Shadows in the Night.

The song comes to a close, Donnie Herron drawing out the final weeping note on his pedal steel and Dylan speaks into the mic, greeting the crowd in Italian before announcing (in English again, now) that they are going to take a short break but will be right back.

While he's gone I notice for the first time that there is a bust on the side of the stage, looking across to where he has spent most of the night at the piano. Perhaps it's Apollo, the

God of Music or Athena (or, when in Rome I should say Minerva), Goddess of the Arts.

During the interval, a man sat two rows in front of me turns my way and for a moment I think it is Sam Elliott. He asks, very slowly, if I wouldn't mind trading my ticket for his paper print out copy, for his collection. Unfortunately, I have my own collection to think about. He rises, as slowly as he talks, and heads off into the crowd in search of someone else to swap with.

The band return fifteen minutes later for the apocalyptic High Water (For Charley Patton). It's dark now and there's a chill wind blowing through the ruins of the Roman empire and the ruins of Dylan's voice.

Here comes the rattle and roll of Early Roman Kings – what setting more appropriate to hear it than this – complete with its Homer reference, and now here is a version of Forgetful Heart that is as beautiful as the venue.

It feels like a very appropriate place to see Bob Dylan; among the ruins of thousands of years old structures, and among all the history they hold. He carries the voice of the ancients with him. A direct line can be drawn back from Bob Dylan to Dante and to Virgil, to Ovid and further back still to Homer; an enduring, visceral and moving use of language that is meant to be performed on stage, not read on the page. When you see Bob Dylan here, it's impossible not to feel the weight of western history moving with him. He is the quintessential American musician and yet his roots, influences and impact are global.

Tonight here in Rome I find myself drawn to him more than ever. Usually I have been bewitched and transfixed, glued to the spot but tonight I feel a power coming from and pulling me to the stage, from the scenery and from the music that I haven't felt anywhere before.

As the band leave the stage at the end of a chilling and spine tingling Autumn Leaves – sung and played to perfection – the power overwhelms me. I leave my seat in the seventh row to move to the rail and to a position as close to the stage as I can get; maybe I'm being led on by the saving grace of Ares, the Greek God of Courage, or Virtus, the Roman deity of Bravery (depending on who you believe in)?

Before the security guards who have spotted me and started heading my way to usher me back into my chair have the chance to intervene, others are joining me and surrounding me and I am pressed against the cold metal rail. Looking around, I can see that the first rows are now all largely empty seats as a crowd of people have followed suit and left their seats to move forward, too. Have they felt the pull of the power from the stage like I have or have they just seen one person rush forward and realise that this was their chance to get closer to the action, as well?

I turn away from the thousands of faces behind me and back to the stage as the band return and play Blowin' in the Wind and then they blow us away with a vengeful, thunderous, funky and dangerous Love Sick. Every twitch, point, every tick, every hop, smile, stare and wince that crosses Dylan's face that by this point I am so familiar with, every note and every nod felt like they were just for me. The song, and with it, the night comes to an end and Dylan is gone; adding a powerful footnote to the history of this ancient venue in this ancient city.

It strikes me that while he plays a mix of rock, blues, folk, torch songs and ballads, dirty grooves and philosophical dreamscapes, there is no one else that plays music like this. The genre is his own. All the influences, all the styles and all the quotes, all the literature and history and the names, the lines from movies, all the apocalypse and redemption that make up his music come together to create a unique sound. No one sings Dylan like Dylan, but more than that, no one writes, rearranges, sounds or plays like him, either.

∞

I'm not due to see Bob Dylan and His Band again until October. He's announced a five night residency at the Royal Albert Hall and so, finances permitting, my plan is to see every show.

Before I cross paths with him again there, I have a couple of opportunities to meet with and talk to some people who either definitely have or have potentially crossed paths with him themselves, starting with Lana Del Rey.

She has a new album out today, Honeymoon, and I'm standing in line outside Rough Trade East just off London's Brick Lane with a friend and a ticket to meet and greet the Ultraviolence singer.

We are at the back of the queue, which takes a couple of hours to slowly dwindle down as fans take all the time they can to talk to, scream at and hug and kiss with Del Rey. Finally it is our turn and as we're the last in line we get to spend a good amount of time chatting with her; talking about what has influenced her writing and style on this record, how it's different from her last one and her hopes for its impact.

Lately a rumour has picked up in the Dylan-sphere online that during the Shadows in the Night sessions last year, he and Del Rey got together to record a duet of Something Stupid. Of course I have to ask her if these rumours are true and so it's disappointing to find out they're not.

"Oh, I fucking wish I'd sung with Bobby," she tells me, and adds that "it's a dream because he's a real hero of mine. But I'd die if we sang together, especially a Sinatra song." She tells me that Dylan and Sinatra are two of her biggest heroes, if not *the* biggest and it's hard not to sympathise with this point as someone who's Frank Sinatra fandom predates even their lifelong Bob Dylan obsession.

All is not lost, though, as she adds "He's just so hard to reach out to, you know? He really keeps himself to himself. I would love to sing with him, just once, though."

We wish her good luck with the album and head off into town. On the way home I clutch a signed copy of the new release to my chest and play the album on Spotify. I get to track nine, Religion, and smile as I hear her sing "all we do is play / all I hear is music like Lay, Lady, Lay".

∞

In my family, Dan Penn & Spooner Oldham's 1999 live album Moments From This Theatre is something of a favourite, so when the pair announce a show at London's beautiful Union Chapel church, six of us go along to enjoy a wonderful evening of timeless music; almost twenty songs, perfectly performed by the warm and soulful artists who wrote and lived them, in a gorgeous room – aesthetically and acoustically –, surrounded by family. It doesn't get much better than that.

Dan Penn was born in 1941, the same year as a certain Robert Allen Zimmerman, and went on to write and co-write some of the most moving and beautiful songs it's possible to have written. That he is not a bigger name having contributed classics such as I'm Your Puppet, The Dark End of the Street, Do Right Woman Do Right Man, I Do, A Woman Left Lonely, Cry Like a Baby, It Tears Me Up, Sweet Inspiration, Like a Road Leading Home and Don't Give Up on Me to the world, and being covered by Aretha Franklin, Charlie Rich, Janis Joplin, Percy Sledge, Otis Redding, Wilson Pickett, Clarence Carter and more is a real shame.

In the late 1960s he teamed up with Spooner Oldham to write together, including on some of those songs mentioned above. Spooner Oldham, like Dan Penn, is criminally underrated and has an understated but powerful way with the keyboard and with the organ like no other.

Sitting behind those instruments, he can be heard on seminal recordings such as When a Man Loves a Woman and Mustang Sally as well as on Aretha Franklin's I Never Loved a Man (The Way I Love You) where he was instrumental in bringing the track to life.

During the I Never Loved a Man sessions in Muscle Shoals, Alabama, proceedings had come to a halt before they even got going. The singer, the musicians and even legendary producer Jerry Wexler had run out of ideas for how to breathe life into the track until Oldham took to the Wurlitzer and came up with the organ part that kicks off the song on the spot. Franklin and the rest of the musicians followed him into the song and upon release the single went to number 1 on the R&B charts, announcing Aretha Franklin to the world as a force to be reckoned with. After they got that first song down, the rest of the sessions flew by without a hitch and the finished album is one of the all-time greats.

Twelve years on from the legendary I Never Loved a Man sessions and Spooner Oldham had been recruited to join Bob Dylan's new touring band. Fresh from recording the Grammy Award Winning Slow Train Coming (also produced by Jerry Wexler in the studio in Muscle Shoals – which must be in contention for being the birth place of more incredible music than just about anywhere else in the world), the first stop for the new band was at the NBC Studio in New York where Dylan had been booked to play Saturday Night Live for the only time in his career. Oldham and Dylan were joined that night by Fred Tackett on guitar, Tim Drummond on bass, Terry Young on keyboards, Jim Keltner behind the drums and Regina McCrary, Helena Springs and Mona Lisa Young on backing vocals to play three songs from the new album.

When the troupe hit the road proper shortly afterwards, the band had expanded and delivered some of the most passionate, powerful and incendiary music ever heard at a Bob Dylan concert. Performing a mix of gospel, funk, blues, rock and soul, no band has ever pushed Dylan to raise his game, to sing with such fervour and conviction as that one did. It's no wonder, considering the musical talent on stage.

Dylan has always been famed for mixing up his arrangements; for not singing a song in the same way twice. On some tours, this was more noticeable than others but it had become a real feature of his live act by 1975's Rolling Thunder Revue, as evidenced by the recordings that preserve the energy (if not the spirit) of that tour. On the first leg in 1975, Tangled Up in Blue is a solo acoustic folk song; by 1976 at a concert in Clearwater it is a fiery rocker, with a different tempo and melody in each verse and a pounding, driving life-force. By the time he hit the road next for the 1978 world tour, the song becomes a luscious, swirling and dreamlike ballad that goes to prove definitively that anyone who ever declared that "Bob Dylan Can't Sing" is plainly wrong.

If that one song could receive so many arrangements over the course of a few years, what Dylan and his band did on the road between 1979-81 was to prove that every song had multiple versions within it. There are so many arrangements of Gotta Serve Somebody, I Believe in You (the live performance from London's Earls Court on June 27th 1981 might be the ultimate trump card in dispelling the Dylan Can't Sing myth), When You Gonna Wake Up, Slow Train and Gonna Change My Way of Thinkin' that you would be forgiven for losing count of them all.

While the arrangements changed constantly from one night to the next, the power and conviction that all on stage brought to them never did.

Back in the Union Chapel in 2015, Dan Penn and Spooner Oldham have left the stage and reappeared at the back of the hall to sell and sign copies of Moments From This Theatre.

While my uncle is talking to Penn and the queue behind us is held up, I spy a chance to ask Spooner Oldham about those Gospel tours he was such a driving force on thirty five years previously. "They were great fun." he tells me, a quiet rasp in his voice. "We played those songs different every night and the key to the tours was rehearsing on stage. We didn't practice all those songs anywhere but in front of the crowds".

∽

There is a thrill in knowing that Bob Dylan is out on the road, a feeling that no matter what is going on elsewhere, that as long as Bob Dylan is doing his thing then the world is at least still turning. Another such thrill is knowing you're in the same city at the same time as him. Knowing that he is all around you, seeing what you're seeing and travelling with you as much as you're travelling with him. Knowing his fans are among you, those of us who move from city to city and country to country following the music.

At the Royal Albert Hall there is an especial buzz that Dylan is in town. It feels like an important moment. He's announced a five night run and all day in my home city there seems to be a palpable energy of expectation for what is to come.

I'm standing outside the stage door on the first night of the five night residency, not really sure what I'm expecting by waiting at this particular spot. No one else has stopped to hang around here, so there is a sea of polka-dot shirts milling past me, looking for the entrance.

While I'm waiting here I look up from my phone and realise that Elvis Costello is stood a few feet away, holding his own phone to his ear and pacing back and forth as he talks. He has just finished up on a project putting music to lost Basement Tapes songs alongside Rhiannon Giddens, Taylor Goldsmith of Dawes, Jim James of My Morning Jacket and another artist, too.

The recordings are entirely missing the charm and magic that was captured by Garth Hudson on the original Basement Tapes in 1967-8 but there are still a few highlights.

Costello walks forward and it feels like he's walking directly towards me. I catch his eye and nod an appreciative nod, which he returns before pulling the phone away from his ear, covering the mouthpiece and leaning my way, "love the boots", he says to me and gestures down at the snakeskin shoes I'm wearing.

I head inside just before the show is due to start and take my seat in the choir. Tonight I'll be sat to the side of the stage, behind the band, which gives a brand new and unique perspective on the dynamics and a new view of Dylan I've not had anywhere else and also a clear view of the rest of the crowd, where I can watch their reaction to the show if I can manage to take my eyes off Dylan & Co.

His piano is angled so that anyone sat facing the stage gets his side profile, while here in the choir we can see him dead on.

That majestic rewrite of Workingman's Blues #2 is gone, replaced as the fourth song of the night by the standard What'll I Do.

Written by the legendary Irving Berlin, back when even Dylan's own parents were still just children, the song's inspiration closely mirrors that of Boots of Spanish Leather; Berlin's fiancée having been sent off to Europe while he sat at home and wondered what he's going to do without her, just as Suze Rotolo would sail for Rome in the early Sixties, leaving Dylan to ponder the same question in their New York City apartment.

Tonight he is singing it as if it's his own song. He is inside it and as he repeats the line "What'll I do, with just a photograph to tell my troubles to?" you can feel all the pain, the loss and the despondency in his voice. I've never heard anyone get so much emotion out of the word "photograph" before.

The next Shadows in the Night song they play is I'm a Fool to Want You. It's one of only seven songs Frank Sinatra ever claimed a writer's credit on. Tonight Dylan claims it all for himself, the age and experience adding a heightened level of regret and self-pity to the title phrase.

The band is playing a lush, slow shuffle – creating such a rich and textured sound for such a small number of musicians and Dylan's voice is soaring, searing. The vibrato and control he has over his phrasing is gorgeous and while I'm here listening to this incredible band, led by this incredible singer, the rest of the world has ceased to exist.

They get through the first bridge and Dylan, intentionally or not, sings "I'm a fool to love you, such a fool to love you" instead of the original "to want you", which only heightens the urgency of the pleading lyrics.

As they finish up on the next song, Tangled Up in Blue, Dylan looks up to the choir where I'm sitting and raises both his arms before turning back to the crowd and announcing the intermission. Perhaps there is someone he knows sitting up here. Maybe he's singing just for them.

The two things I'm enjoying the most so far tonight are the unique view of Dylan at work and the introduction of more and more Great American Songbook standards. In Rome he played two, but tonight that has been expanded to five, to six, to seven; each with carefully and beautifully delivered phrasing and extended notes.

At the end of Autumn Leaves and the main set, Dylan again points up to this section of the choir and then, to really make the point, lifts both his hands in appreciation our way again before heading off stage to get ready for the encore.

∞

Night two, and I'm supposed to be coming with a friend. They text to say they can't make it anymore. I'd recently told them that the likelihood they were about to witness the first performance of I and I for sixteen years was close to zero, so perhaps that's where their interest cooled.

While I'm returning to the Royal Albert Hall alone, there are at least other friends to be seen here.

I meet Diane in one of the ground floor bars; a friend from various Dylan groups on Facebook, she's been on the road with Bob her whole life and I'm sure has her own wonderful stories to tell. More fans, John and Steven of those I recognise, and a host I do not, are gathered together chatting about last night's show and one of them quizzes me on the view I had from the choir.

Further into the bar is a man who goes by the name Hollis Brown. A legendary bootlegger, his YouTube channels are a goldmine of Never Ending Tour footage. He's a gentle giant of a man, long hair poking out of his brown wide brimmed hat. He sells me a spare ticket for the fifth and final show of the residency and I thank him for all the videos he has shared with the world and wonder how many times he's seen Dylan live, and how many magic moments he's captured.

I have a box all to myself tonight in the loggia tier, giving me a clear view out across the gorgeous hall to the stage where from the first note until the last, Dylan reminds me that when you're in a room with him, you're never actually alone.

∞

The third night's performance is drawing to a close. Each night so far he's played largely the same setlist, with The Night We Called it a Day replaced by Full Moon and Empty Arms last night, and the former returning tonight.

My mum and I are sitting in the stalls this evening so it feels like I'm working my way around the room over the course of the week and getting a full 360° perspective of the show. This, by far, is the closest I've sat to him so far.

After that haunting rendition of Autumn Leaves to close out the main set I notice that Dylan and his band are leaving at a stage exit right by where we're sitting, a few seats in from the aisle.

I tell my mum to grab her stuff and she asks if I mean to leave to go and wait outside by the tour bus as I'm already on my feet, bustling past the people who have returned to their seats after giving Dylan a standing ovation. I want to get closer to Dylan without having to miss the two song encore, though, so lead her to stand against the steps that look down over the stage entrance and exit just in time to see the group returning for the final flourish.

All through Blowin' in the Wind and Love Sick I'm nervous that security are going to ask us to either return to our seats or stop blocking the stairs, but no one comes and the gig is over.

As the band leave the stage for the final time, Dylan is leading the way and other bodies have joined around us now, cottoning on to our plan to get a final glimpse of him, leaning and stretching their hands over the edge hoping that he will reach out and touch them. My mum and I stay still exactly where we are and Bob Dylan locks eyes first with her and then with me. He nods his head to us and keeps on walking out of sight.

Those baby blue eyes, immortalised in Joan Baez's transcendent 1975 hit Diamonds and Rust, are as piercing as a blade and as deep as the ocean. Just as his voice contains a lifetime of experience and living, so do his eyes when they're looking right at you.

He had a bemused look on his face, one eyebrow lifted and the shadow of a smirk crossing his mouth, as if to ask what was going on here? What was all the fuss? As if he hadn't just brought the house down with an incredible performance. As if to say "Oh that? That was nothing. I'm just getting started and the best is yet to come".

As we walk back through the night to London Victoria I get lost in thought. I'm thinking about the night of January 31st,

1959 when young Robert Zimmerman saw Buddy Holly in concert at the Duluth National Guard Armory.

Three feet apart, young Dylan was mesmerised as he locked eyes with the Heartbeat singer.

Tonight, 56 years later, I am feeling the exact same way.

∞

All through the fourth night I keep thinking about that briefest of moments when we looked each other in the eyes at the end of yesterday's show.

Instead of playing The Night We Called It a Day or Full Moon and Empty Arms he sings the Jimmy McHugh and Harold Adamson tune Where Are You? tonight; the only song from Shadows in the Night where Dylan's delivery steers away from sentimental and into bitterness and frustration.

It strikes me that Shadows in the Night could act as a sister piece to 1975's seminal Blood on the Tracks; both covering ground of loss and love, loneliness and regret, the more recent album the result of time healing the wounds that were more immediate and open on the former.

During tonight's version of Spirit on the Water the band get locked in a groove they haven't found so far on the run of shows. A new pathway has obviously revealed itself to them, collectively, because as if by magic they all follow in the same direction and get taken along down the new instrumental melody on the outro to the song.

There are two beats on the snare of George Receli's drum and then at first it seems it is Dylan and Donnie Herron, always in sync, who take the first steps on the pathway and within a bar or less, Charlie Sexton, Stu Kimball and Tony Garnier have caught up in step with them and they swing into a new rhythm that only those of us in the room will ever get to witness.

It is moments like this, and it is not the only one I have noticed through the night, that make it worthwhile returning night after night. The song titles might look the same written down on paper, but it doesn't reveal the secret that every night they sound different.

∞

It is the final night of the five show residency. It's going to be strange waking up tomorrow and not looking forward to returning to this stunning venue in the evening; going to be strange waking up in the morning and having to find something else to do with my day rather than spending it with Bob Dylan.

I take my seat down on the arena floor, completing the set for areas I've seen Bob Dylan from at the Royal Albert Hall; gallery, choir, loggia, arena and stalls.

At the interval I head to the bar and bump into Mick McCarthy, the football manager who is currently in charge of Ipswich Town. You meet all sorts of people when you're following Bob Dylan around.

When I mention the fact that we had a picture of him and my mum together on our fridge in my childhood home from the day that he opened the Primark in our hometown of Bromley, he regrettably informs me that he doesn't remember my mum specifically but does at least remember the Primark opening and explains he was involved because of his friendship with the owner of Penneys in Ireland, the clothing giant's parent company.

I grab a drink and return to my seat humming "It's hard times in the country, down on Penny's Farm", a folk song that inspired at least a couple of new songs by the artist we're here to see tonight.

He returns to the stage for the final time this week. The applause all night has been thunderous. At the encore a man rushes forward towards the stage from the back of the arena, but with such a run up he has less luck in starting a swell towards the stage as I did in Rome and the security are on him in a flash. He is dragged back to his seat as the show rolls on.

I know I am not the only one who had been here for every show and the buzz that was in the air at the start of the run has grown to fever pitch as the week has gone on.

Not only recognising the people who have been here all week, football managers or musicians, I've started to spot familiar faces from the gigs I've seen abroad, too. There's the tall, long haired man I've seen in Rome and Sweden, who is always sporting a cowboy hat and boots as well as a moustache that means you could easily confuse him with Sam Elliott's character in The Big Lebowski; the man who in Rome he asked me to exchange my printed ticket for his paper one; but there are other standout characters that you see wherever you go, too – the woman who never buys a ticket, walking up and down the queue outside every venue begging for a spare ticket and somehow always making it in; those who have a never ending supply of polka dot shirts that they wear in country after country and those who clearly just love having a good excuse to travel as well. Each of us are on our own Never Ending Tours.

∞

A week later and I'm in the car with my Grandad, heading down to Southampton from London.

He, and indeed all my family, were born and raised in the city on England's south coast, and together we have been making this short journey plenty of times a year to head to St Mary's Stadium to watch our beloved Southampton FC, most recently just two days ago to watch a 2-1 win over Aston Villa in the League Cup.

This time, though, we're going to be watching Bob Dylan and His Band for the final UK date of this year's tour. As soon as the date was added, I knew we couldn't dare miss it.

The venue is run down and ramshackle, indeed, I don't think I've ever been to a venue on this scale that had carpeted floors before and if there weren't so many bodies standing in the room I'm sure we'd be able to smell the years of beer and sweat that are ingrained into the floor of Southampton's O2 Guildhall.

Dylan takes to the stage and I'm struck by the thought that this is a bizarre place for him to perform, let alone close out his UK tour. Surely not since March of 1964 when The Rolling Stones played here has anyone of this stature been on the bill.

I wonder what he makes of this city that I've spent so much time in; whether he spent the day checking out the old city walls, first erected in 1180 and still standing or if he quenched his interest in boats with a walk around the city's docks. I also wonder what leads him to book performances in places that are not usually on the tour path of major icons such as him, places like Midland, Texas or Moose Jaw in Canada, Wollongong in Australia and here in Southampton. He is the embodiment of the wandering troubadour, bringing his songs and performance to every corner of the globe.

Tonight he is decked out in black and white cowboy boots, black trousers with blue embellishments down the sides in place of his usual white stripe, a blazer that is stitched with a gorgeous, webbed and floral pattern in the same blue and a wide brimmed cream coloured hat. He's getting cooler with age, which says a lot for a man who is referred to as *the* style icon of the 1960s.

In recent times, Dylan has looked to the legendary Manuel Cuevas and Jaime Castaneda for his tailoring. Cuevas created the suit that Dylan wore to play for the Pope in 1997 and has continued to work with him since, curating his now signature riverboat gambler stage look.

Part Civil War General with the stripe down his leg and part flamboyant roving troubadour with the jacket embellishments, Dylan's look completely suits the music he performs around the world – it is a look and a sound from another time and place, and a look and sound that is completely his own.

To my ears he's sounding better and better as he ages, too, which considering he was also *the* musical icon of the 1960s as well, is an even more impressive feat.

CHAPTER FIVE
I COULD HAVE TOLD YOU

Forest Hills Tennis Stadium. Queens, NY. USA. July 8, 2016

On August 28, 1965, Bob Dylan played his first live show featuring an entirely electric half; laying the foundation for the formula he would employ on his now legendary tours of '65 and '66 by opening his show with a solo acoustic performance before returning after the interval with a backing band (incidentally, flipping the order from his then most recent album Bringing It All Back Home which opens with an electric half and closes out with a four song acoustic run).

He'd famously angered the folkies at the Newport Folk Festival a little over a month previously by daring to step onto stage to perform three songs with an electric guitar and band. Depending on what you read or listen to, the boos were either for the volume, the choice of instrument, presence of a band on stage, for the fact that the finger-pointing protest songs had been eschewed for more introspective numbers, or for the fact that the performance only lasted for about twenty minutes.

No matter what the exact issue was, they all became recurring complaints at each of the one hundred and sixteen shows that he performed over the year and a half after Newport.

The first of those shows was at Forest Hills Tennis Stadium, a 14,000 seater arena located in Queens, New York. Surely the fans who packed themselves into that outdoor show in late summer 1965 weren't too upset about the lack of protest songs as they can be heard on surviving tapes of the show howling with appreciation at the opening lines of She Belongs to Me, To Ramona and Love Minus Zero / No Limit. For this crowd, it seems that hearing Dylan accompanied by only his acoustic guitar is enough, whether he was singing about the lonesome death of Hattie Carroll, the guns and clubs in Oxford Town or the vagabond who's rapping at your door.

By the time he debuts Desolation Row the crowd is rapt and hanging on every word. They catch all the humour and wit; they laugh, applaud and cheer and roar at the absurd and surreal images and one can only wonder at the dreamlike experience of hearing this song live for the first time and having no idea what is coming next or for how long it's going to go on for – it was not officially released on the wider world until Highway 61 Revisited made its appearance in record stores two days later.

The acoustic half is drawn to a close with Mr Tambourine Man and the crowd have kept up with Dylan every step of the way, he's cheered off stage and takes a fifteen minute break to allow the audience to work themselves into a mob as they watch the road crew set up the stage for a full band performance.

At Newport he was joined on stage by Mike Bloomfield – a ferocious and frighteningly talented guitarist whose solo work is highly underrated – Al Kooper on the organ he so famously played on Like a Rolling Stone despite not yet being an organ player, Jerome Arnold on bass, Sam Lay on drums and Barry Goldberg on piano.

By the Forest Hills show, only Kooper remained and after a half time pep talk from Dylan who told them that they needed to be prepared for anything and that anything could happen, is joined onstage by Robbie Robertson on guitar, Harvey Brooks on bass and Levon Helm sat behind the drums.

As they hit the stage after the break, all hell breaks loose and the respectful cheers and clapping of the crowd is replaced by hostile shouting, booing and whistles that on the remaining recordings of the show drown out the music being made on stage. It's hard to tell that the second half starts with Tombstone Blues, the crowd is that loud.

When the now electric intro of I Don't Believe You (She Acts Like we Never Have Met) gives way and Dylan sings the first line the audience groans because the song used to go like *that* but now it goes like *this*.

Dylan and his assembled band are unrelenting. Whatever the audience throws at them, and indeed by all accounts there actually were a lot of projectiles aimed at the stage, they match it with a wild and raucous showing and the seeds are here for what is to come on the following world tours where Dylan and co take on all comers from all the corners of the globe.

It wasn't just projectiles the band had to worry about. Some folk fans seemed to take matters into their own hands by climbing onto the stage and trying to pull Kooper and Helm from their seats and instruments, leading Dylan to quip that it was like the "attack of the Beatniks around here".

Towards the end of the hour long set it seems Dylan's insistence that this is his new sound almost wins over the crowd – the opening lines of It Ain't Me, Babe drawing both groans and cheers and a wild hollering at the chorus where the audience splits itself in half to sing along and boo in equal measure.

By the time the show wraps up with Like a Rolling Stone, the cheers are drowning out the jeers and everyone seems to join in with a singalong chorus; Dylan may feel he can put Newport behind him. He's won this battle but the war was just beginning.

∞

It's March 2016 and Bob Dylan is releasing the dates for his summer tour. He's announced a concert in Chicago in June and when I see that Mavis Staples is supporting him (incidentally, this first announced show is in Staples' hometown), I know immediately that I can't miss this tour. I've been watching the dates trickle in every day waiting for a particular venue or city to jump out at me.

And there it is. I've not been kept waiting long as on March 7th, a show at Forest Hills Tennis Stadium is announced. It will be the first time Dylan has played there since his first electric gig fifty-one years ago in 1965. Of course, his official website makes no mention of this detail but it's not lost on the local press or ticket promoters.

Dylan has a long history with Mavis Staples and The Staple Singers. He first heard their music drifting in on the waves of his radio in the late 1950s. He would sneak it into his room at night and hide it under the covers, turning the volume down low and the dial anywhere that would pick up a signal from some far off world (usually Shreveport, Louisiana) to hear the sounds of Hank Williams, Johnny Cash and eventually, The Staple Singers.

Later he would recall hearing them for the first time, "Pops had kind of a gentle voice. But then this other voice came on, which I found out was Mavis. One of the first songs I heard that made my hair stand up on end was called 'Sit Down Servant.' That just made me stay up for a week after I heard that song."

A few years later they crossed paths for the first time, at a concert in New York in September of 1962.

Apparently the Staples' were "shocked this little white boy – and he was little – knew our stuff". By then, Dylan had started to write the songs that made him famous as a protest singer, Blowin' in the Wind and Oxford Town or Masters of War, and the lyrics caught the attention of Pops who told the rest of the band to focus on what he was singing. A year later, they recorded a cover of Blowin' in the Wind, becoming the first non-folk group to release a song written by Bob Dylan.

Also in that year, Dylan tried to act on his crush on Mavis by proposing to her, or rather, to her father. On telling Pops Staples while backstage at the Newport Folk Festival that he wanted to marry Mavis, the older singer replied loudly enough for everyone in the vicinity to hear "Don't tell me, tell Mavis!"

Of course, the pair never wed and the next time they appeared on a bill together was at the tail end of 1976 for The Band's Last Waltz concert. It was another sixteen years before they crossed paths again, Staples as one of the all-star backing band behind Dylan as he performed Like a Rolling Stone on the 10th Anniversary celebration of David Letterman's late night talk show.

In 2003 the pair got together to record a playful, bluesy cover of Gonna Change My Way of Thinking for a tribute album to Dylan's Gospel period and not long after the pair both embarked on separate tours in Tokyo. Dylan happened to be staying in a hotel across the street from Staples and phoned her up to come and hear his new album, which eventually became known to the world as Modern Times. Talking to Rolling Stone a few years later, Staples tells how she had to turn down the offer, "I said, 'Bobby, I can't come out. It's after 1 a.m. in the morning. I can't come out by myself in Japan.'"

After everything they've been through together, from the March on Washington and a proposal to missed connections in Tokyo, they're hitting the road together for a twenty-seven show tour. The fact that I am going to see them in Bob Dylan's New York, and at the Forest Hills Tennis Stadium no less, makes it all the more exciting.

※

While Robert Zimmerman was born and raised in Minnesota, Bob Dylan is a New Yorker.

His first six albums were all recorded in either Columbia Records' Studio A or Studio B at their plot at 799 Seventh

Avenue. He played in just about every coffee house that would have him in Greenwich Village, most notably the Café Wha? and Village Gate; lived on West 4th Street, spent time in The Folklore Center run by Izzy Young on MacDougal Street, made The Washington Square and Chelsea hotels his own and forever tied his young image to Suze Rotolo and Jones Street on the cover of The Freewheelin' Bob Dylan, so being booed in his adopted hometown in 1965 must have hurt.

At 19 years of age, he first arrived in a snow covered New York on January 24, 1961, and by April 11 he was playing his first notable gig, at Gerde's Folk City, opening for the legendary bluesman John Lee Hooker.

In September of that year, Dylan was invited by fellow folk singer Carolyn Hester to play harmonica on her new album, the first she would record for Columbia Records. She'd been signed a year previously by the legendary A&R man and record producer John Hammond, who was introduced to Dylan at this session and went on to sign him, too.

John Hammond was born in New York in 1910. His impact on the music industry is immense, and the landscape of popular music would look a lot different if he had decided to live off his mother's Vanderbilt and W & J Sloane fortune, instead.

He was passionate about music from an extremely young age, trying his hand at both piano and violin before the age of ten, and it was a passion that never left him.

On weekends when he was supposed to be heading into the city to continue his education, Hammond set out his own curriculum by heading to Harlem and supposedly watching artists like Bessie Smith, before later dropping out of the education system altogether to move to Greenwich Village and become a journalist with Melody Maker and a DJ with the WEVD station (the latter for no pay, as well).

Another driving force behind this incredible man was his interest in social and civil rights; perhaps unexpectedly so for a (white) man growing up incredibly rich in early 20th Century America, and this informed his movements in the music industry.

Hammond wrote in his autobiography that he heard no colour divide in the music, and his actions back up his words; he influenced Benny Goodman to start working with black musicians at a time when this was not happening and arranged a couple of concerts in Carnegie Hall in 1938 and '39 dedicated to highlighting and empowering black music. Shortly after these shows, he invested in and booked artists for shows at Café Society – America's first racially integrated night club.

He would continue to champion black artists and music for his whole life, whether by signing the artists he loved to the major label he worked for or writing about civil rights issues extensively.

As a talent scout and A&R man he is unrivalled; Hammond is credited with discovering Billie Holiday, Aretha Franklin, Count Basie, Benny Goodman, Leonard Cohen, Bruce Springsteen and, of course, Bob Dylan.

Just imagine what music would sound like today without the ear, attention and integrity of John Hammond.

Mavis Staples steps up on to the stage amidst a light rain that has seen those who have made it to their seats in time pull out an array of brightly coloured hooded waterproof ponchos. She is a beam of light amongst a grizzly evening and the bright floral pink cardigan she's donning is outshining even the most garish of those waterproofs.

I cannot believe that there are so many empty seats around us as she launches into If You're Ready (Come Go With Me), a Staple Singers classic. Those of us who are here on time are most certainly ready to come go with her anywhere she leads over the next hour or so.

She is two year's Dylan's senior but she is youthful, warm and radiates an overwhelmingly positive energy. Her guitarist Rick Holmstrom is no Pops Staples but he's locked onto the groove and Staples and her band have us on our feet almost instantly.

Mavis Staples has been singing songs of hope, equality, love, peace, understanding and faith her whole career. She started singing with her family's band in churches in 1950 and she is still bringing the message with her and converting any unbelievers as the venue starts to fill up. You would hope that at this stage of the game, and with a crowd such as Dylan's in front of her now, that she is preaching to the choir.

Her voice is in impeccable shape; her trademark rasp full of life and full of soul as she sings the lyrics to Take Us Back, a new song from her triumphant recent collaboration with Jeff Tweedy, Livin' on a High Note.

In between songs she is funny and conversational; she has sections of the crowd laughing and mock-booing as she jokingly asks how the local baseball team (The New York

Mets) have been performing lately before adding, with her tongue planted firmly in her cheek, that she asks because she always loves to hear how The Yankees are doing.

She covers The Talking Heads and then instructs the crowd to keep an eye out for the way that Bobby walks during his set, saying that no one moves the way he does (of course, she is right).

The Staple Singers first recorded For What It's Worth in 1965, the same year Dylan was booed out of Forest Hills, and tonight she treats us to a fantastic version.

The seats around us are all full now and the sunshine of Staples' voice has blown the clouds away.

She closes out her part of the show with a funky, soulful I'll Take You There. She already has.

∞

We've spent the few days in Manhattan before the show exploring Bob Dylan's New York, or moreover, *I've* spent the time dragging my friend around the landmarks.

Our first stop was into Greenwich Village to check out The Café Wha? where Dylan sang as a young folksinger; The Bitter End where he set up camp in the mid-seventies to plot and plan the Rolling Thunder Revue and to the steps of 161 West 4th Street where he shared his first New York apartment with Suze Rotolo, moving in at the tail end of 1961. The brownstone building features the trademark New York fire escapes latticed along the front fascia and is now neighboured by a tattoo parlour and a sex shop. It's all very Greenwich Village.

I try to find Bleecker Bob's, the famous record shop, one

street along but it seems since I last came here in 2012 it's closed down so we settle for a wander around the similarly named Bleecker Street Records but find nothing that catches our eye. We do at least make friends with a beautiful grey cat called Creeper who has made an old crate it's bed, downstairs.

Back on the street and we head to another of Dylan's former apartments, 94 MacDougal Street, where he returned to the Village after a spell away with his family upstate in Woodstock. It was probably here that A. J. Weberman made a name for himself by rummaging through Dylan's rubbish for reasons that only he can explain.

We walk through Washington Square Park where there are a couple of people with guitars and some shouting from atop the boxes they've brought along to stand on, but mainly it's just tourists like us passing through.

We head past the Hotel Chelsea, currently closed for renovations, where Dylan claims to have stayed up for days writing Sad Eyed Lady of the Lowlands for his wife Sara in the mid-60s. The Hotel Chelsea, of course, has a whole musical history of its own, masterfully detailed by Sherill Tippins in Inside the Dream Palace.

Uptown, we check out Carnegie Hall where Dylan played his first concert proper in 1961. He played there five more times, finally in 1968, making an at-the-time rare public appearance to perform at a Woody Guthrie memorial concert, backed by The Band.

Outside of the obvious Bob Dylan landmarks in New York, there are quite a few other things to see and do in the city, too. We head up the Empire State Building, walk through Central Park and at the other end of the island,

Battery Park with its views of Ellis Island and the Castle Clinton National Monument.

We grab an amazing, indulgent and filling vegan breakfast at Terri's and eat it while looking up at the Chrysler Building through their window. It's not a bad view for a café to have, as far as they go.

Walking around again, I find that the city has changed a lot in the four years I've been gone. Not only has Bleecker Bob's been lost to time, but so have the Virgin Megastore and Toys'R'Us from Times Square.

There's an uneasy tension all around, this time, too. We walk past the garish and obnoxious Trump Tower on 5th Avenue and there is a protest taking place outside. Presumably the presidential candidate is in town, and all the circus that comes with him.

We hop an empty Staten Island Ferry to pass by the Statue of Liberty. What she represents seems entirely at odds with the beliefs, actions and values (or rather, lack of) of the business tycoon who is hoping to become the next Commander-in-Chief.

We've explored every corner of Manhattan in search of Dylan history but managed to explore the city for itself, as well.

Tom Waits once said that you don't need to be busy in New York; New York will make you busy. And indeed it has for us as we walk through Central Park and stumble upon Radio City Music Hall and wander around Rockefeller Plaza; visit the Freedom Tower, stand at Canal and Bowery and try to squeeze in as many vegan meals as our stomachs can bear – whether they're at Brooklyn's Champs Diner for the best vegan junk food in the city before a slow walk back across the iconic suspension bridge, or at the upmarket Dirt Candy of Manhattan's Lower-East Side.

Each New York neighbourhood has its own distinctive character and feeling. Not just Greenwich Village or Harlem, but the Bronx, Williamsburg, Brooklyn and Queens, too. It's to the latter that we're sat on the train to now, on our way to the show tonight, surrounded by a cocktail of broad New York accents.

∽

As has become the norm, Dylan has kicked off the show with Things Have Changed. It is ringing out into the open air. Everyone who is just filing into the arena floor in time to catch the opening song remain on their feet and those of us who were already here have risen to join them.

This song has transformed from a rollicking threat when I first heard it into a steady, languid manifesto. Once it was moving so fast it felt like it could fall apart at any second but now it is a steady and powerful opening statement.

Between songs back at the Apollo in 2011 or in Philadelphia in 2012 there was a wild and untamed cacophony as the band warmed up their instruments while the lights were out. Here it feels like the opening notes of Things Have Changed are still ringing as the band kicks into the new insistent, marching beat arrangement of She Belongs to Me, the only song still in Dylan's regular setlist from his 1965 gig here. Throughout the song, those around us begin to take their seats and settle in for the night ahead.

Dylan blows through his harmonica for the first time in the evening and is given a whooping seal of approval from the audience. A bend of the knee, a final blow of the harp, a half turn and nod towards George Receli and the song comes to a halt.

This time there is a short gap between the songs while Dylan heads to his piano and after one more nod they launch into a rolling Beyond Here Lies Nothin', which could easily have been what it felt like the last time he left this venue fifty one years ago with the boos still ringing in his ears.

Next up is a five song run that showcases the Bob Dylan of the present, and future. The Night We Called it a Day from Shadows in the Night is followed by Tempest's Pay in Blood before they play a note perfect rendition of Melancholy Mood from his latest studio outing, Fallen Angels.

When Duquesne Whistle was first introduced into the live show the short intro that kicks off the song on Tempest was not to be heard but here it comes today as the band warm up into the song. A few people around us are on their feet ready to shuffle along to the swinging rhythm and we get up to dance, too. Our seat is on the aisle and so we step into the space to have more room to move; almost recreating the moves from the music video, the moves that this song demands you make to it.

Halfway through the song, though, security come and usher us back into our seats and instruct us to enjoy the show from there, and not from our feet.

Next up is another Great American Songbook song that isn't on either of the two standards albums that Dylan has so far released, That Old Feeling, most famously and gorgeously recorded by Chet Baker in 1954.

Tangled Up in Blue comes and goes, the same arrangement the band have been using for the last few years but Dylan has resurrected an old set of re-written lyrics.

I'm sure I'm not the only one who is hoping for at least *some* acknowledgement from Dylan of the venue he's playing at tonight and at the song's end we get it, in true Dylan style.

He grabs a tennis racket from atop his piano and waves it aloft as he announces the intermission. We are not to get an acknowledgement of Dylan's own history here but he does at least remind us of the other use for this venue.

∞

Throughout his career Dylan's sense of humour has been continuously overlooked while an aura of seriousness, contemplation and chilliness has been built up by those who interview and write about him.

His wry sense of humour not only permeates his lyrics all the way back to The Freewheelin' Bob Dylan but he has also been known to slip 'Dad Jokes' into his band introductions from the stage – "we were nearly late for the show tonight, we got a flat tyre. There was a fork in the road" – or into his Theme Time Radio Hour series – "I was nursing a drink in Elmo's the other night, when a termite walked in and asked me where was the bar-*tender*?" -, into his 2003 film Masked and Anonymous and his eye for satire made it into his visual work in The Revisionist Art series in 2012. He even finished his MusicCares Person of the Year acceptance speech last year by announcing through an enormous grin that "I'm going to put an egg in my shoe and beat it".

Whether he's yelling about liking Fidel Castro (and his beard) to scare off a farmer in Motorpsycho Nightmare or clueing a reporter in when asked what his songs are *about* in a 1966 interview that "Oh, some are about four minutes; some are about five and some, believe it or not, are about eleven or twelve", Dylan's sense of humour is often ignored.

His delivery of lines such as, when leaning into Tom Petty during the Traveling Wilburys recording sessions as George Harrison walks by, "you know, he was in *The Beatles!*" was so deadpan that in hearing the story re-told, a lot of people don't know whether he was even joking or not.

When Peter Green introduced himself to Dylan at a party in L.A in 1971 as the "manager of Led Zeppelin", Dylan quipped back "Hey man, I don't come to you with my problems, now, do I?".

"Love and Theft" contains a knock knock joke; a quip about a politician wearing jogging shoes so they can run for office, Dylan singing about sitting on his watch (so that he can be on time) and his paraphrasing of the Groucho Marx line about calling down to room service and asking them to send up a bigger room.

The image that is made up of Dylan as cantankerous and curmudgeonly or as a man who never smiles or seems to enjoy his time on stage, is a wild misrepresentation of a performer who is a lot more lively, jocular and light-hearted than he is made out to be.

Watching him smiling and dancing between words and notes on stage every year for the last five years has left me wondering which shows the commentators who say he never looks happy on stage have been to.

Clearly, those reviewers weren't present at his show on July 15, 2013 in Toronto's Molson Amphitheatre when he brought Jeff Tweedy and Jim James onto the stage to join him on the blues spiritual 12 Gates to the City, before leading the audience through a two verse sing-along section of the song, smiling all the while.

Perhaps they missed his show in Barcelona in 1984 where Dylan lets the crowd take over every chorus on Blowin' in the Wind, yelling "all right!", "OK!" and "uh-huh!" between each of their lines, calling for them to sing it again "one more time" (twice).

Or in Brazil 28 years later, when he let the crowd sing the choruses on Like a Rolling Stone, clasping his hands to them in admiration at the end. In between these shows and countless others like it, after another audience sing-along Like a Rolling Stone, this time in Edinburgh in 2004, Dylan told the crowd "I must say, you're the best singing audience we've ever heard."

Evidently the critics who say Dylan doesn't have fun on stage or interact with his audience missed his November 12, 1996 show in Dubuque, Iowa, where Dylan instructed security to let any fans on stage who wanted to climb up before spending the last fifteen minutes of the show dancing and swaying, chatting and hugging with all those who did.

The critics who say that Bob Dylan is a grumpy old man clearly haven't heard the stories of the numerous times he visited his grandson's school to give acoustic performances to him and his classmates; the times he took a break from touring in Belfast and Buenos Aires to visit the children's wards of the hospitals there to hand out harmonicas or the time he sat by Little Richard's hospital bed for weeks on end in the mid-80s and even paid for his hero's medical bills, the time he gave Ke$ha a hug backstage at the Firefly Festival in Delaware, in 2017, to make up for her Seinfeld red carpet snub and nor do they remember or acknowledge that all the proceeds from his Christmas album continue to go to homeless shelter charities around the globe.

He doesn't seem to take himself or life as seriously as people make out that he does, and the glint in his eye and smile on his lips as he's waving the tennis racket around onstage at Forest Hills shows that a lot of thought has gone into this visual gag. It was all worth it.

∞

During the intermission a couple of older heads turn to us and tell us that it's great to see younger people in the crowd enjoying Dylan and his music.

Moving into my twenties, now, I see a lot of Dylan fans online who are younger than I am. The timeless nature of his art, his lyrics and his constant recreation makes him a timeless performer. He has something for everyone. Indeed, the latest albums he's released, the Standards albums, will connect with a generation even older than he is and the music of his youth have become standards themselves. He has a body of work that stands up and connects with any generation and will continue to do so for as long as people are listening to recorded music.

We don't get to talk for too long though as here come the band, straight into High Water (For Charley Patton), Dylan bobbing and weaving on the spot during the song.

Why Try to Change Me Now is another Songbook tune, written by Cy Coleman in 1952, but tonight it could be a personal manifesto from Dylan. At this late stage in the game, why would you want to change him at all?

He plays another unreleased standards tune; I Could Have Told You. It is heart-breaking. It is hair-raising and it feels like he's stopped time with this one. Some of the audience clearly aren't here to hear him sing obscure Sinatra era covers and are milling about, heading to the bar or the bathroom until a Dylan original is up.

To me, he has climbed inside these songs to the extent that even if this one was written more than half a century ago by Jimmy Van Heusen, it is a Bob Dylan song now. Donnie Herron's gut-wrenching pedal steel takes the place of what would have been an orchestra in any original recordings and Dylan's weary and worn voice is cracked and ageing in all the right places as he sings of regret and lessons learned from love gone bad.

All too soon it's over and done with and the band kick into a lively Spirit on the Water, its infectious riff weaving its way into my brain. By the time he lets us know he can't go back to paradise no more for killing a man back there, the audience is bursting for the next line, almost daring him to sing it. When "you think I'm over the hill?" leaves his lips, the crowd fires back with a heavy "No!" and repeats the response a moment later when Dylan teasingly pushes the point further, "you think I'm past my prime?" Fifty-one years ago the crowd here might have given him a less enthusiastic response to the questions.

We remain seated for the rest of our show until first Long and Wasted Years and then Autumn Leaves draw a standing ovation from the crowd. During the encore break everyone surges forward towards the stage and stays transfixed through Blowin' in the Wind.

There has been a spate of racially motivated shootings

throughout the country over the summer, including within the last week that we've been here in New York, and it feels as if Dylan is singing with extra conviction when he asks the crowd how many deaths it will take until we know that too many people have died.

Love Sick is the song that closes out the show tonight and after the uncommon intensity of Blowin' in the Wind it feels like a drop in energy. Where last year in Rome this was a rocker that threatened to topple the ruins behind him, tonight this is a slow burn and Dylan sends us off into the night on an understated note.

∞

On Friday, October 7th, 2016, Bob Dylan took to the stage at the Desert Trip Festival in Indio, California in front of a 75,000 strong crowd.

He kicked off the weekend's festivities with Rainy Day Women #12 & #35. By the time Roger Waters closed out the event with Comfortably Numb, The Rolling Stones, Neil Young, Paul McCartney and The Who had also all taken to the stage.

Initially the festival was due to take place on one weekend but presumably due to demand the so called "once in a lifetime festival" had a second weekend added. In between the two events, Dylan was (I believe, rightly) awarded the Nobel Prize in Literature for "having created new poetic expressions within the great American song tradition".

Controversy never seems to be far away from Dylan and upon the announcement there was no shortage of outrage online from the literary community; from people who don't seem to like his music or those who didn't like the fact that he took two weeks to acknowledge the award (in an interview with Edna Gundersen of The Daily Telegraph discussing his then latest art exhibit).

The only people whose thoughts on the matter actually matter, ultimately, though, are those of the Nobel Committee and once an award is granted it can't be rescinded.

The thing with being a Bob Dylan fan is that it becomes a big part of your personality, a big part of your life and it becomes a part of what makes you who you are. When the news broke he had been awarded the coveted prize, friends and relatives began to text me to congratulate me as if I had personally won.

To close out his second performance at the Desert Trip festival Dylan opted to play Why Try to Change Me Now?. In the light of his freshly minted Nobel Laureate-hood and the magnified dissection of his life's work that came with it, it was a very fitting question to ask, indeed.

CHAPTER SIX

STANDING IN THE DOORWAY

Stockholm Waterfront. Stockholm, Sweden. April 1, 2017
London Palladium. London, England. April 30, 2017
Wembley Arena. London, England. May 9, 2017

Bob Dylan's next gig is in Stockholm, the home of the Nobel Committee. Surely he is going to collect his medal before one of the shows.

He skipped the Nobel banquet in December, citing "pre-existing commitments" but sent on an eloquent letter of gratitude which was read out to the night's crowd by the Ambassador of the United States to Sweden, Azita Raji. Patti Smith performed A Hard Rain's A-Gonna Fall at the ceremony.

As soon as I see that he is playing this concert I book a seat in the very front row.

∞

At a private ceremony before the show Dylan did, indeed, pick up his medal. I wonder if it's going to take pride of place on stage with him tonight, next to his Oscar for Things Have Changed, next to his prayer beads and the bust of Athena.

Here outside the Stockholm Waterfront there are fans scattered about everywhere. I've not seen this many fans outside a venue so far ahead of its start time before, by lunchtime the venue's carpark is full and there are people all around. There is a small camera crew walking through the crowd interviewing people, and a lot of uniformed road crew with headsets milling about the tour buses.

Inside Dylan is meeting the Academy. He is disguised in a black leather jacket, hoodie, gloves and biker boots.

Later, Klas Östergren will tell the Associated Press that the proceedings went well and that Dylan is "a very nice and kind man". Sara Danius, who made the announcement in 2016 that Dylan would receive the prize and who is the first female Permanent Secretary in the organisation's history, later expands that "Spirits were high. Champagne was had. When he had the golden medal in his hand, he turned the backside up, looked at it for a long time and seemed amazed".

On the reverse of the medal is an engraving that depicts a poet listening to and writing down the song of a Muse playing a lyre. In the modern era, no performer can claim to have had the muse sing in and through them quite as much as Dylan.

While the world has been discussing Dylan's merit as a Nobel Prize winning literary figure, he has released another new album of covers. Triplicate is made up of thirty Great American Songbook standards and broken down into three albums of ten songs each.

Some fans want him to return to singing his own songs by now and dismiss the record out of hand but I didn't play anything but this album on the plane from London to Västerås or on the coach from Västerås to Stockholm.

As we drove through a never ending spruce-tree forest, the hazy light flickering through the sea of trim trunks, Bragging and It's Funny to Everyone But Me, My One and Only Love and I Guess I'll Have to Change My Plans flicker through my ears. Perhaps these are the finest of Dylan's Songbook performances; they are looser and more relaxed than the previous two albums but that looseness is borne from a total inhabitance of the material.

The first of his standards records, Shadows in the Night is a perfectly crafted album. Fallen Angels is overlooked because it is not Shadows in the Night (although the performances are for the most part just as good). Triplicate is dismissed because it is an overindulgence, but if you ignore what came before and just listen to the music it's hard not to appreciate the singing, the playing and the lyrics.

At the Stockholm Waterfront, Nobel Medal in his possession, it isn't any of the so-called Sinatra covers that steal the show, it isn't any of the four 60s songs that are clinging on to their spot in the show but the first performance of Standing in the Doorway since 2005.

At first I don't recognise it. From the instrumental intro I can't figure out what song is about to be sung. I'm not expecting this song to be anywhere near the setlist so even at the opening line it takes me a while to realise what is going on.

These are the moments we come for.

∞

We settle into the front row of London Palladium's uppermost balcony. Thanks to the legendary bootlegger Hollis Brown I had a pre-sale link for tickets but even then the best seats near the stage had been snatched up by the time I logged on.

The clamour to see Dylan only grew and outside the venue, Argyll Street and the nearby Carnaby Street were awash with fans and the air was buzzing with chatter. Plenty of them stood at the doors to get a picture underneath the marquee of the famous venue with an even more famous name lit up across it.

The Palladium, of course, has a storied history of its own. It was first opened on Boxing Day in 1910 and was nearly demolished during World War 2 when, twelve days before Dylan was born, an unexploded German parachute mine was dropped through the roof, becoming lodged above the stage and threatening to explode.

At the close of the war, the venue became a premier venue for performances by huge American stars such as Bing Crosby, Frank Sinatra, Ella Fitzgerald and Judy Garland.

In the 1960s, the British invaded the venue which saw performances from The Beatles, The Rolling Stones, Cliff Richard and Petula Clarke on the television show Sunday Night at the London Palladium.

During his Nobel Banquet speech Dylan alluded to the fact that when he thought about where his songs should be performed, he had the London Palladium in mind. This run of shows is the first time he has ever played here.

Things Have Changed sets the tone for the night ahead. With a new arrangement, the song is now slower, more pronounced yet more menacing and ominous than in recent years. Before it had been a riotous rebel-yell, Dylan breaking free from his shackles.

Now it is portentous. It is a warning and it is subtly threatening. He used to care but things have changed and now there's no telling what he'll do.

Dylan looks bigger than he ever has before; he always commands the room and even if you want to watch the rest of the band it's hard to take your eyes off him. Tonight he is mountainous and filling up every inch of the stage.

The band lilts into the Southern country waltz of To Ramona. Before Dylan even starts singing a roar of approval goes up from the crowd.

The lights are low so the room is smothered in a warm glow. There are huge halogen stage lights high above the band's heads, smaller lamps around them and a rippled curtain acting as a stately backdrop. It feels more like we're here to see a play than a gig, with the props around the stage. Perhaps that is what is really going on tonight.

Dylan's voice is rising and falling, pushing his remaining upper register at times and sliding down to his lowest notes masterfully. He plays a piano line that matches his cascading vocals throughout and the song ends with a final flourish on the keys.

The lights drop and the band descends into a bluesy chaos, each of them riffing on their own in the dark. Suddenly George Receli hits his drum and the band immediately lock into step. The lights return and Dylan launches into a rocking, shuffling Highway 61, taunting and teasing as he drags out every last line of each verse.

Chaos reigns between each verse. Dylan hammers the

piano like a man possessed and the band stay in step with him the whole way. The bedlam continues into Beyond Here Lies Nothin', the border-town rhythm holding place as the band shuffle through the verses but as Dylan's ascending piano line leads them into the instrumental breaks it feels as though every instrument is playing its own song, somehow keeping it together despite walking such a tightrope.

For the final break, the song modulates and all hell breaks loose. The chaos is overwhelming. It feels like Dylan and His Band have opened a portal to another world where anything goes.

The next song to ring out from the darkness is I Could Have Told You; Donnie Herron's aching pedal steel slicing mournfully through the air before the lights come up and Dylan is standing centre stage, holding the microphone stand with both hands so that it is raised from the floor as he bends to sing beautifully into it.

The next songbook tune to be played is Melancholy Mood, following a roaring Pay in Blood. Charlie Sexton usually rings this one in with the same notes he played on the record but tonight he is confidently adding new flourishes, searching for the light and shade in the melody and playing with a jazzy style I've not heard behind Dylan since he duetted with Wynton Marsalis almost fifteen years ago.

While Sexton plays, Dylan stalks the stage. Left to right and back again, waiting for his moment to step into the spotlight. He sways, hand on hip and steps up to the microphone.

After nearly a hundred and fifty performances, this song is more Dylan's than ever. He is no longer crooning it as he did when it first entered the setlist, now it's a growl. It's a graveyard shuffle that wouldn't be out of place on Tom Waits' Rain Dogs album. Dylan finishes his part and lets the microphone stand go, which teeters while he struts away as if he had nothing to do with it in the first place and Sexton closes the song out in the same way he opened it.

Dylan can barely make it back to the piano before His Band have launched into the swinging parlour intro of Duquesne Whistle. The hazy lighting and Dylan leaning at his piano makes it feel as though we're in an Old West Saloon with Dylan at the bar and the band about to burst into Dixie at any moment.

The next song is one that I wanted to hear Dylan singing ever since he began singing the songbook tunes, Harold Arlen's Stormy Weather. Dylan's stormy voice is perfect for the song and tonight it is a treat to hear it live.

So far tonight I have been transfixed. There's something about this room, something about the way the lighting is setting the mood and something about these arrangements that is kicking off a heat that I haven't experienced before at a Dylan show or anywhere else. It feels as though I'm watching a ghost show; it's not really here in front of me but an apparition of a concert that has always been happening just out of sight, such is the spirit that the band have tapped into this evening.

During the next song, somehow, impossibly, things kick into another gear.

It's the same arrangement of Tangled Up in Blue that they've been dragging around the world for a few years now. Dylan stands centre stage with the microphone stand draped across one hip and his hand on the other, occasionally flicking his hand out in dismissal. He hops from one foot to the other, twists his cowboy boot and dances through the melody. George Receli kicks the band on with an understated urgency and the volume creeps up.

Charlie Sexton takes another solo that sounds like there are three guitarists playing at once. Dylan poses for a while and then swaggers over to the piano and as he starts improvising around the melody the volume rises again before dropping way back down as his vocals come back in.

This band are so perfectly in sync with each other that these changes seem to happen telepathically; including Dylan there are six master musicians on stage but when they play together, they become one. They are no longer Bob Dylan, Tony Garnier, George Receli, Charlie Sexton, Donnie Herron and Stu Kimball, they are simply one autonomous band.

By the time Dylan is halfway through the final verse, by the time he's done casting off all the people he used to know, the rhythm and volume have hit heights they hadn't previously reached in the song and his voice cracks to be heard over the music as he cries out that he's still on the road looking for another joint. It is a true imperfect moment; it is a true perfect moment. One piano flourish later and the song is done.

I think it's safe to take a breather and sit back in my chair as the opening riff of Early Roman Kings kicks in. I feel that having heard this song so many times now, I've heard every way they can possibly play it.

Dylan proves me wrong, tonight, though. His voice becomes cavernous, imposing itself on every inch of the room. He is digging out a new, descending melody that breathes fresh life into the song, the room and everyone in it.

Between the verses Dylan beats his piano up and gets back to singing; he ain't afraid to make love to a bitch or a hag and by the sounds of things, he ain't afraid of anything else, either.

When he quotes Homer's threat to strip us of life, strip us of breath and ship us down to the house of death I can feel the weight of three-thousand years in the lines, and Dylan captures every second that has passed in that time in this incandescent, unconquerable vocal performance. He brags that there'll be no one else we'll want to see at verse's end and he's right.

After a performance such as that, it's little wonder the crowd are so vociferous in their protests when Dylan sings about being over the hill, past his prime on the evenings next number, Spirit on the Water.

After a sombre Love Sick where I can't tell if it's the arrangement or the come down from the songs before it that make it feel subdued, Charlie Sexton takes the lead again for the intro to All or Nothing At All.

Dylan saunters back to centre stage, walking lightly on his toes and swinging his arms widely. He grabs the mic stand and takes up a spot at the back of the stage next to Sexton.

He places a hand on his hip and, with feet firmly placed on the ground, turns his torso to face his lead guitarist, who mirrors Dylan's movement exactly in time.

At the end of the solo, Dylan nods to Sexton and they both swing back to face the crowd with comically exaggerated movements; Chaplin-esque in their way and

Dylan launches into a vocal which is halfway between his crooning Sinatra voice and the rough growl that preceded it.

As with Early Roman Kings, Desolation Row tonight is sung with a whole new gravity, a whole new spirit and a whole new conviction; Dylan finding a hidden melody within the song that is unlike any other iteration I have ever heard before.

By That Old Black Magic I'm in a spin and loving the spin I'm in. This performance has never let up, even for a second, in intensity or passion. There's no longer an intermission halfway through the show and perhaps that has helped Dylan kick on from the burst of energy that opened the performance and not let it slip away by interrupting the flow.

However he is managing to summon up the spirit and the energy for this performance, I am in awe. Dylan has fifty-four years on me but I am exhausted just watching him strut across the boards, watching him battle his piano and watching him dance, hop and pose when he is dragging his mic stand about centre stage.

He presses on with a scorching Long and Wasted Years, a tender Autumn Leaves and Blowin' in the Wind and a ferocious Ballad of a Thin Man, which closes out the greatest gig and performance I have ever seen in my life.

∞

In February, my uncle, my grandad and I were in the crowd at Wembley Stadium as Southampton played in the League Cup Final. Manolo Gabbiadini was robbed of a hat-trick by one of the worst off-side decisions you're ever likely to see as we lost the match 3-2 to Manchester United.

Tonight my uncle and I are repeating the journey to Wembley. There will be no disappointment tonight, three months on, when Bob Dylan and his band hit the stage at the Arena.

As we're walking the wide pathway from the station to the arena I cast my mind back ten years to when my uncle first introduced me to Bob Dylan; I cast my mind back to hearing Subterranean Homesick Blues for the first time, to listening to Modern Times together upon its release. To watching The Other Side of the Mirror together and Don't Look Back, No Direction Home and scores of bootlegs of Dylan's Saturday Night Live and Letterman appearances.

I think about how without all those formative experiences I wouldn't have been to Philadelphia, to the Trädgårdsföreningen or the Terme di Caracalla; I wouldn't have been to the Forest Hills Tennis Stadium in Queens and I think about the adventures that are still yet to come but which wouldn't have been, without the introduction in my eleventh year.

As I walk into the venue with the man who introduced me to this world, it feels as though we are Bringing It All Back Home.

CHAPTER SEVEN
CLEAR THROUGH TENNESSEE

Gran Teatre del Liceu. Barcelona, Spain. March 30, 2018
Tivoli Theatre. Chattanooga, TN. USA. October 28, 2018
Tennessee Theatre. Knoxville, TN. USA. October 31, 2018

It's the Easter weekend and I am sitting in an otherwise empty box at the Gran Teatre del Liceu in Barcelona watching Bob Dylan and His Band play, elevating this from a Good Friday to a great one.

This venue is simply stunning. It opened its doors here on La Ramblas in 1847 and has a capacity of around 3,000. The hall somehow manages to feel both intimate and cavernous. The detailing on the faraway ceiling is breathtaking and the circular layout of the room makes it feel like the seats are all closer to the stage than they probably are.

Much like the Terme di Caracalla this historic building is primarily used for opera but tonight Dylan is commanding the stage, opening with that striding and forcefully mid-tempo arrangement of Things Have Changed. The shadows of the band and their instruments on the curtained backdrop are long and tall and they flicker like ghosts performing to the hall.

His focus is slightly off compared to the fiery shows I saw last year. It may have been ten months since the show at the London Palladium but I can still feel the earth shattering power of Dylan's performance that night rattling around inside me. I can still recall at will the haunting echo of his voice on Tangled Up in Blue and Early Roman Kings from almost a year ago as if I was hearing them for the first time whenever I happen to be thinking about them.

His attention tonight, at times though, seems to be elsewhere. Perhaps it is because this tour so far has been marred by technical and sound troubles.

On March 27, in Madrid, his microphone cut out midway through Thunder on the Mountain. The band played on and Dylan didn't let the lack of amplification deter him; he carried on singing and is just about audible on the tape of the show hollering along through the final verses. That he can be heard at all feels staggering; his 76 year old lungs allowing him enough power to be heard without a microphone above an amplified five-piece band.

At the end of that song the band left the stage and the road crew took to it to try and address the problems. Ten minutes later Dylan returned to perform Blowin' in the Wind before cutting the show a few songs short.

A night later and the issues had not been resolved. This time the power went down earlier in the night's proceedings and on a fan shot video Dylan can be seen having fun leading the crowd through an un-amplified clap-along and sing-along version of Desolation Row. It must have been an absolutely unique and almost surreal moment for anyone who was in attendance and is testament to Dylan's desire for the show to go on come rain or come shine.

There are flickers here and there tonight, too that the speakers are on the edge of blowing. As the volume has crept up through the show, there has been a flicker of crackle and a few pops as the band push the speakers to their limit.

It adds a level of suspense to the show that is outside Dylan's control. There is an edge in the atmosphere in the room, too, so presumably most of the crowd are aware of the technical troubles the tour has faced here in Spain.

Thankfully so far, though, the power has remained on throughout despite its warnings that at any minute things could change. What seems to be more distracting to Dylan tonight is the fact that his striped trouser leg won't stay over the top of his cowboy boot and between each song he is bending over to fuss with it and straighten it out. Every time he sits back down at the piano, though, the leg pops back up over his boot and the game begins again.

During Early Roman Kings the audience are ready to play their part. When Dylan instructs anyone who sees him coming to wave a handkerchief in the air in surrender a group of five or six along the front row leap to their feet, shout "¡Olé!" and wave a white handkerchief each above their heads in response.

During the next song, more of the audience try and clap along to the beat of Desolation Row; to tease Dylan into a repeat of the Madrid show but tonight he hammers away at the piano and rolls along with the vocals without even acknowledging the audience participation.

There are a few new lines in Long and Wasted Years. Never in my life did I expect the phrase "what a blithering fool he took me for" to escape Bob Dylan's lips, live or on record, but tonight, at least that's what I think I hear him say. There's a bit of a new arrangement, too, as that insistent guitar motif occasionally gives way to a teetering and staggering turnaround before the band kicks back into the next verse.

If the band have pushed the sound system and speakers so far tonight, on the next song they push them all the way to the limit. Thunder on the Mountain is, well, thunderous.

From the new riff that opened the song to when George Receli kicks in and powers the band into the opening verse, the song has been at fever pitch and as it goes along it just ramps up further and further. Dylan spits out the lyrics with a conviction and purpose that has been missing from the rest of the show. The speakers crackle and threaten to cut out. Perhaps the power coming from the stage sparks new life into them because they hold out and the volume seems to step up.

Receli is beating his drums like his life depends on it and the band are all locked in tight together. Dylan sings about his soul expanding, walking the hard road down, a mean old twister bearing down on him and how all the ladies in Washington are scrambling to get out of town. There's a fire on the moon and there's a fire in the room, too, as the song comes to life. It feels like it's too much to maintain and could fall apart at any moment and when the band drop out one by one I feel like it has, until Receli takes a drum solo and the band vamp back in for a final flourish.

I'm out of breath from just witnessing the performance so can only wonder how those on the stage are still standing, not entirely spent from it. It would have been worth the cost of flights, accommodation and tickets alone just to have witnessed that one song.

Twenty years after it opened, this venue was severely damaged by a fire and had to be closed down for repairs. Thirty years on again, in 1893, two bombs were thrown from the balcony by anarchists, forcing the venue to keep its doors closed until the following year.

Just over one-hundred years on from the bombing and the building burnt down again, this time the fire damage so severe that the opera house couldn't reopen for a further five years.

Tonight's performance of Thunder on the Mountain was so loud, so powerful, vengeful and forceful, the heat kicking off of the stage and out of the speakers so white hot, that I would not be surprised if yet further repairs need to be made to the Gran Teatre del Liceu after the show has finished.

While the lights are still out and the crowd catch their breath, Donnie Herron's pedal steel cuts through the blackness and casts a spell across the room. The first notes of Autumn Leaves piercing through the residual rock and roll of Thunder on the Mountain.

Dylan has switched gears and now stands centre stage to sing, note perfectly, his haunting and sombre take on the Jacques Prévert – Joseph Kosma – Johnny Mercer ballad. It couldn't have been further from the song before in terms of energy, but it's just as captivating, just as powerful. Thunder on the Mountain had the room physically moving but Autumn Leaves is hitting somewhere much deeper within.

Dylan, as a singer and performer, contains multitudes.

The show has finished and I am standing outside the Gran Teatre del Liceu on La Ramblas. There is a chill wind blowing up from the beach where earlier in the day I sat in the Barceloneta Sangria Bar, eating vegan tapas; cruelty-free calamari, plant-based shrimp and sipping on sweet, fruit filled red wine.

There is a huge crowd gathered here, all of us standing between the stage door and Bob Dylan's tour buses. Charlie Sexton is leaning against the stage door, one hand pressed to the wall and the other dragging a cigarette to his mouth. He's been chain smoking for the last ten minutes.

Occasionally fans call out his name and each time he looks up and smiles or nods but no one approaches, out of respect and reverence. We're all waiting for one last glimpse of Dylan before the night is through, but he's likely already made his exit. Earlier in the day there were two buses parked out here but now only one remains.

Eventually the stage door swings open and the crowd edge forward and murmurs swirl in the air. Stu Kimball is first out and is met with a cheer and cries of "Bravo!". He throws a plectrum into the waiting crowd and turns to check that the rest of the band are behind him. George Receli is next out, a small white towel around his neck.

Charlie stubs his cigarette out and joins in step with Tony Garnier who is smiling, nodding and waving to the adoring crowd. Donnie Herron takes up the rear and the door closes behind them. They head through the gap in the crowd, right past me. Having seen them I decide it's time to head back to my hostel and try and push through the crowd which had clamoured around the band but has now become a mess of people heading in all directions.

I'm pushed about by the mass of bodies; half of them trying to follow the band and half of them heading home, like me.

I look up and realise that I am walking directly behind Donnie Herron who has the rest of the band right in front of him. I can see Charlie Sexton stepping up onto the tour bus, followed by Tony Garnier and finally the multi-instrumentalist, Herron. As he steps up onto the bus I can spot a route out of the crowd opening up but a man blocks the path and holds his arm out, ushering me onto the tour bus.

I look at the step, at the man's outstretched arm and finally up to his face. A look of confusion flickers through his eyes and he speaks in a heavy American accent, "I'm sorry. I thought you were with the band. You can't board this bus, sir."

If only I hadn't looked up and had confidently stepped on-board! The mistake was not one he would have had to apologise, to me at least, for.

As if that wasn't surreal enough, once I finally make it through the crowd I find myself stopped again. I've been tapped on the shoulder and turn to see a man a little shorter than I am staring at me, his brown eyes wide open. "Please may I have your autograph?" He asks in an accented voice.

I ask him why he would want *my* autograph, of all people. "You're Beck, no?". No, I tell him. Beck has about twenty-five years on me, but it's dark out so I'm not taking offence at that. He apologises and we get talking. It turns out that he has travelled in from Latvia and this was his first Bob Dylan concert. I ask him how he enjoyed the show and he says very much and enthuses about having heard It Ain't

Me, Babe and Tangled Up in Blue live. He is coming back tomorrow night and is already dreaming of further concerts beyond that. He asks if I'm coming back tomorrow and I tell him that unfortunately not. I have other plans in the city for the rest of my stay but it is enough to know that I'm sharing the air, the space and the atmosphere here with Bob Dylan, His Band and his fans.

―

There is a part of me that is wishing I had booked tickets to see the second show in Barcelona, too. I'd been due to be travelling here with company but at the last minute the plans changed. If it had been just me coming here the whole time there's no doubt I'd be in the crowd again tonight.

Instead, I'm walking around the small yet impressive structure of the city's Natural Science Museum.

There are long rows of glass cases filled with crystals and minerals, ethereal rocks that look like they are too beautiful to have come out of the ground.

I was hoping to see more bones and relics of long extinct animals than there are on offer, but the complete skeleton of Gastornis – a pre-historic flightless, carnivorous bird that fed on the early ancestors of the horse and other small mammals in the Paleocene – is a fascinating artefact.

Outside on the streets of Barcelona, more recent and yet no less fascinating, are the works of Gaudi dotted around the city on plenty of buildings.

The Casa Milà, Casa Batlló and La Manzana de la Discordia buildings around the city give Barcelona an entirely unique, dreamlike and captivating personality; as do the Park Güell – which is well worth the painful journey and steep climb to reach – and the more conveniently located, commanding and unfinished structure of the Basílica de la Sagrada Família.

If Park Güell is dream-like, then the summit of Mount Tibidabo is a trip. It's an even more arduous journey, a long hard climb – the Funicular del Tibidabo train that brings you here never filling you with confidence that it will be able to scale the severity of the hill – and once you reach the top you are greeted with the most stunning view of the city, but also by a towering and imperious church-upon-a-church. If that isn't surreal enough, turning around to face the other direction and you're greeted with an amusement park, complete with rides with their original 1899 mechanisms intact.

I'm not sure whether the train up here or the Ferris Wheel at the summit felt less reliable and more perilous, but both of them manage to get your adrenaline pumping without even picking up any real speed.

My final stop is one to see another great artist, synonymous with the city: Lionel Messi at the Camp Nou as Barcelona take on Real Madrid in El Clásico.

From outside, the stadium is hideous. Where was an artist with an eye like Gaudí's when these huge, grey and lifeless concrete slabs were being erected? Inside is something different. With a beautiful view over the pitch, the city beyond the lip of the stadium and a towering mountain range beyond that it is easy to forget that there is a game of football taking place below me.

Lionel Messi is the greatest artist the game has ever seen and he creates space for himself without even breaking stride, even when surrounded by four or five opposition players. Tonight he scores a penalty but the game finishes 3-1 to Real Madrid (Marco Asensio stealing the show for Los Blancos) and, with it, my time in Barcelona comes to an end.

∞

I'm walking up Kensington High Street on my lunch hour. It's May 25th and the sun is shining, the street is busy and I'm in a hurry to make it back to the Warner Chappell office before the end of my break.

As I pass the McDonalds I see an eccentric figure step out of The Ivy, a much more up-market chain than the one I've just passed. He has leather trousers on, a heavy blazer, long curling black hair and beard, small round sunglasses and a wide brimmed hat. I would recognise this unique look anywhere.

As I step forward towards him he looks up into my direction so I nod and stop to say hello. Work can wait.

After confirming that he is, indeed, Don Was (of *course* he is, no one else looks like this), we get chatting and I tell him that I appreciate his work on the underrated 1990 album Under the Red Sky.

Under the Red Sky comes at the end of a misunderstood period in Dylan's career. Almost universally panned, it contains some beautiful lyrics, some fantastic songs and admittedly some real filler. Always written off as a drop in form after the year before's return to form Oh Mercy, Under the Red Sky has at least a lot more merit than Knocked Out Loaded and Down in the Groove.

Even those two albums, though, are not without their charm. Brownsville Girl on the former is a career highlight from a career full of highlights. The rest of the album could be said to be made up of songs that only a fan would love, but that would be to dismiss You Wanna Ramble, Maybe Someday, Got My Mind Made Up and Under Your Spell.

Down in the Groove may be my least played Dylan album of all time but at least has Had a Dream About You Baby, Silvio, Shenandoah and Rank Strangers to shout about.

Before those two albums came Empire Burlesque, boasting some of Dylan's finest songwriting of the decade. With better production, songs like Tight Connection to My Heart (Has Anyone Seen My Love?), I'll Remember You, When the Night Comes Falling From the Sky and Dark Eyes would have been regarded as classics, such is the strength of their lyrics. (The strength of these songs is demonstrated where Dylan always produces his greatest work: on stage.)

Back on Kensington High Street, I have to ask Don Was about the most recent session he worked on with Dylan, recording He's Funny That Way for the Record Store Day exclusive Universal Love – Wedding Songs Reimagined.

I tell him that I'm aware he probably can't say much, but he is happy to share *something*, at least.

"Bob is the best; I love working with him." He tells me, "just watching him is something special, you know? He did that recording right up in front of the orchestra with no headphones on. He got it in a couple takes. It's not his style but he nails this stuff."

He was coy about saying any more, but it was nice to have had the curtain pulled back even slightly at all. I ask what he's doing in town and he tells me he's here to see The Rolling Stones and asks if I've seen them before. I've not, I confess, and he tells me I need to change that and catch them while I can.

When I get back to the office I impulsively buy a ticket from another fan for their show that same night at The London Stadium.

I meet the man I'm buying the ticket from and head inside the stadium. I've been here to see the football before and the atmosphere that the West Ham fans muster is atrocious; with any sound and energy lost to the gaping open air and making all my previous trips here a drab affair.

I hope the atmosphere is better tonight but all through the opening set from Florence + The Machine I'm beginning to worry it won't be. The stage is enormous and I've never seen as many speakers staring out into a crowd as there are here tonight and yet the sound is dreadful. It is drifting over our heads and it's hard to make out one song from the next. The mix is horrible and the vocals are barely discernible above the music.

Those worries are immediately cast away the second The Rolling Stones rock up on stage and launch into Jumpin' Jack Flash. Miraculously the sound is now perfect. It's a gas. I wonder whether some efforts have been made to keep the opening act sounding poor so that the main event blows us away.

The first thing I notice is that it is *loud*. Just the way a gig should be. Keith Richards is prowling the stage, effortlessly cool and in his own world; playing some of the finest rock riffs ever written or recorded.

Charlie Watts sits behind the drums, holding the whole thing together as Mick Jagger runs from one side of the stage to the next doing his best to rewind his clock, trying to outrun his seventy-five years.

Standing among the 60,000 other fans while the Stones rattle and roll through their greatest hits is exhilarating. After a wild and raucous run of Let's Spend the Night Together, It's Only Rock and Roll (But I Like It) and Tumbling Dice my adrenaline is pumping.

Next up is a track from their most recent record, 2015's Blue & Lonesome. They went back to their roots here and covered twelve classic blues songs and in the process sounded more vital, vibrant and engaged than they had in decades.

It is one of only two occasions this evening that they play a song released after 1981. When you have songs to pick from like Miss You, Wild Horses, (I Can't Get No) Satisfaction and Dead Flowers, it's understandable that you'd want to find space for them in the setlist but it feels strange that the fourteen studio albums they have made since the early 80s are only represented by two songs.

One of those is The Worst. Mick Jagger introduces the band and then heads off stage for a quick outfit change, leaving Keith Richards to step up to the microphone and take centre stage.

He's the coolest Rolling Stone by far and when I think of what the band are and what they mean, I think of him. Like Dylan, he is totally immersed in his art. He is steeped and dripping in music history. Like Dylan, he lives and breathes his work.

He leans into The Worst, teasing the intro out of his acoustic guitar and letting his voice sound as old as he is.

There's a realness and a tenderness to his singing; there's a little heartbreak in his voice. That realness has been missing throughout the rest of the show, which is no bad thing, but while Mick Jagger has spent the night doing his best Mick Jagger impression, Keith Richards just *sings*.

On The Worst and his next song, the electric, forceful Happy, he flirts around the melody; sometimes singing it the way he does on record and sometimes drifting on by. I like that he is going with the song, he's singing it how it goes now. How it goes tonight. Not how it went before when it was first laid down.

For all the greatest hits, for all the incredible music and all the showmanship, for me, the best part of the night is when Richards takes centre stage and just plays.

After the show has finished and I'm walking back to the station, surrounded by fans in all directions, there is a carnival atmosphere in the air. Everyone is drunk on the energy and vibrancy that was kicking off the stage.

There is a different energy here to any I have felt walking out of a Dylan gig, where his crowd speak in hushed tones of reverence or complain that they couldn't understand what he was saying or that he didn't play Tambourine Man.

Perhaps it comes from having 60,000 other fans around you pushing the atmosphere up, perhaps it comes from hearing a greatest hits selection performed largely as they were on the records that are so ingrained in all of our minds.

It strikes me that so many times I've seen Dylan perform and only play a handful of songs from the 60s and 70s and how I wouldn't change that. He's giving us a performance based on where his art is *now*, who he is in 2018, not who he was in 1965.

But I also wouldn't change The Stones' performance tonight. They haven't released a record as strong as "Love and Theft" in the 21st Century so it doesn't make sense to drop Brown Sugar to hear She Saw Me Coming.

If Keith Richards ever wanted to head out on the road solo, though, and sing more songs like The Worst, You Don't Have to Mean It, You Don't Move Me, Love Hurts and Take It So Hard then I would be the first to get in line.

∞

Four days later and I have traded in the excess of the London Stadium for the comparable intimacy of the Royal Albert Hall.

I've seen Dylan here six times but tonight I'm here for someone else. Someone who is forever tied to the Dylan story but who is an incredible artist, singer and performer in their own right and who was all those things before anyone knew the name Bob Dylan.

Joan Baez is in the spotlight. Her shadow dances on the wall behind her and her small band are beautifully underpinning her masterful guitar playing. Her voice has only gotten better with age, which is saying something considering where it started out from.

This year she has a new record out and she plays its title track, Whistle Down the Wind. I can't think of many more haunting, affecting songs that have been released so far this year, or for a long time before that.

It is a cover of a Tom Waits song but like so many covers

that she has performed down the years, the song now belongs to her.

Dylan, of course, hangs heavy over the night with four of his songs performed (Farewell Angelina, It's All Over Now Baby Blue, Seven Curses and The Times They Are A-Changin') as well as Diamonds and Rust, Baez's masterpiece which was written about him.

But when she sings, it doesn't matter who wrote the songs. Whether it was Tom Waits, Bob Dylan, Woody Guthrie (Deportee), Kris Kristofferson (Me & Bobby McGee) or Robbie Robertson (The Night They Drove Old Dixie Down), what matters instead is the voice that is singing the songs and the guitar she's playing them on.

∽

By the time the autumn turns into winter, I realise what a busy year of music I've had. Dylan in Barcelona, The Rolling Stones twice, Courtney Barnett a few times and Burt Bacharach, Rodriguez and Joan Baez; Jeff Tweedy and Nick Cave, The Arctic Monkeys, Tony Bennett, Patti Smith, The Lemon Twigs and more.

I've been given tickets to see Tom Odell tonight, too, and in the morning I'm boarding a plane to go and see Bob Dylan again on my biggest solo adventure yet.

∽

Before he introduced me to Bob Dylan, my uncle had played me Tony Joe White. He always made me copies of the albums that I loved the most from those he'd shown me; Millie Jackson, Candi Staton, Albert King and with Tony Joe White he'd made copies of Black and White, ... Continued and The Train I'm On. They spun so frequently in my Walkman that every song was seared into my brain before long.

We spent hours together watching Tony Joe White: Live From Austin, TX on DVD and as a ten year old who had no idea what Polk Salad was, whether it did or didn't rain in Indianapolis in the summer time or who Roosevelt and Ira Lee were, I was transfixed. I didn't know those things, but I *did* learn from him that even trolls love rock and roll, that there were only ten more miles to Louisiana and that mamas shouldn't let their cowboys grow up to be babies. But that was another place and another time.

In 2016 I saw Tony Joe White at the Union Chapel in London. At the end of the gig I sat alone in the wooden pews as the crowd filtered out and I thought back to all the times I'd listened to him before, and how that was what I'd really been listening to that night as he took to the stage with just his electric guitar and harmonica.

On my way out of the venue I bumped into him and got to express my gratitude for the lifetime of music he'd released that has moved me so. Despite us being the same height, he was a giant, bear of a man. This late in the game he was frail and his energy for talking seemed to be drained by the evening's performance, but he didn't need to say any more than the words that he'd sung over the course of the previous hour and a half.

This is what I'm thinking of as I sit in the airport in Atlanta, Georgia, looking out over the planes landing and taking off. I'm waiting for a connecting flight to Nashville.

After turning my phone on for the first time since take off in London nine hours ago, I'm greeted with the sad news that Tony Joe White has died, aged 75.

I'm looking through the glass and a light rain is closing in on the runway. It's raining here in Georgia but it feels like it's raining all over the world.

∽

I've dropped my bags off at the Drake Motel. Apparently Elvis Presley stayed here, once, in another lifetime. In 1999, a TV movie – Blue Valley Songbird – starring Dolly Parton was shot here.

It does not feel like the kind of place you'd expect to find a King or the Queen of Country. There's a pool in the centre of the courtyard complete with a fountain half-heartedly sprinkling away. At this time of year, only the bravest, or most foolish, of souls would bother to take a dip.

The room feels ragged and dirty, but it's more from age and wear and tear than from neglect. It has character and it has spirit. I bet a million people have forgotten memories left behind in the rooms of this motel.

I'm sure that outside I hear a rattling gunshot, but it might just be my mind playing tricks on me for being so far away from home and on my own, too.

The dark is rising and so I grab my phone, the room key and head out into the night, ready for the show.

It's halfway along the four mile walk that I realise how tired I am. This morning I was in bed in London and now, via Atlanta, I'm walking through downtown Nashville, Tennessee.

The main strip is a neon dream, a hustle and bustle that has one cowboy boot in the past and one in the present. People are everywhere, taking up both sidewalks and the road. I keep walking past, not here to stop in any honkytonk or saloon.

It's less than a week until Halloween so every square park I pass has been decorated with scarecrows sat atop hay bales, carts overflowing with cobwebs and pumpkins, wooden broomsticks resting by their sides.

Finally, I make it to the Marathon Music Works and join the queue. It's a warm night, the air is fresh and the moon is casting shadows on the ground. There are two tellers at the front, selling off the remaining tickets for the night. One of them points at me and beckons me forward, despite there being about three or four people still ahead of me in line.

They turn around to face me and I look around, too, wondering why I've been singled out or if actually there's someone behind me who is being asked forward. I step towards the counter and the ticket seller asks for my name, which catches me off guard but I tell her and she looks down a list. I already know it's not going to be there because I haven't bought a ticket yet. "I can't find you, would they have put you down under anything else?" she asks, so I explain that I don't have a ticket and will be needing to buy one. She blushes and tells me that she had assumed I was with the band so was checking the guestlist, and that I'd have to re-join the back of the line for general admission.

Despite the brickwork fascia, the inside of the venue feels like a converted barn. The standing area for the crowd is surrounded by bars and merch stalls, and it feels a little cramped. This venue can hold just over 1,500 people and as we're all closed in and squeezed together it feels like there are as many people here as the room can hold.

The opening act closes up, Waxahatchee treating us to a mix of old and as-yet-unreleased tracks, and now the wait begins for the main event.

I'm almost out on my feet by the time that Courtney Barnett hits the stage but with every thrash and hammer on her glittering red Fender Jaguar, she is bringing me back to life, summoning an energy reserve I didn't know I had.

It seems that she is having a similar effect on the rest of the room as you can feel the people around me come alive when the line they most relate to or the song they feel the most deeply comes and goes. There are a lot of people here tonight, like me, on their own.

Courtney Barnett's music is the perfect companion to put an arm around you and make you feel less alone, and so it goes tonight as she sings on the second song about friends who treat you like a stranger and strangers who treat you like a best friend or on the anxiety anthem Avant Gardener one song later.

Next up is the scathing Nameless, Faceless where she addresses the fears that women face every day due to the violence and aggression of men; whether it's online or in the physical world. Within the song is perhaps the greatest artist-critic takedown that I can think of, too.

An online troll responded to her first album with the quip "I could eat a bowl of alphabet soup and spit out better words than you", which Barnett sings verbatim in the songs second verse, before stepping away from the mic and wryly adding with a shrug, "but you didn't" and carrying on with the song.

On I'm Not Your Mother, I'm Not Your Bitch she gets *dark*. The lights flash blood red and her guitar's overdrive goes into overdrive. She growls the lines more than sings them and by the end of the grungy, punk-esque number, the growl has turned into a scream and eventually a roar and then the music is gone, cut dead seemingly in the middle of a note, a thought, a spell.

After a more sedated number and then a slow, winding introduction to Small Poppies the fire and brimstone is back. During one instrumental break, Barnett is down on her knees with her head leaned so far back that it's almost touching the floor as she shreds out a violent, shattering, vengeful solo on her guitar.

I can't work out whether her presence, her lyrics, the new arrangements to these songs and the way they are transformed for the stage or her guitar playing is the most impressive thing tonight, but whatever it is, the performance is devastating and transcendent. There is a conversation going on between those on the stage and those of us in the crowd tonight, and it is beautiful.

There's an audience singalong for Depreston and Elevator Operator, and between the volume-testing and raucous rock music she slips in a couple of acoustic covers; Houses by Elyse Weinberg and Gillian Welch's Everything is Free, but they don't feel like covers. Right here and right now, she is making these fragile and beautiful songs her own.

The night closes out with an incandescent Pedestrian at Best, a thank you shouted into the adoring crowd and then I'm back on the street and dead on my feet. The energy that was flowing from the stage and keeping me upright has been lost to the crisp night air.

Sitting in the cab I think that the gig would have been worth the trip alone but that's not what I'm here for. Bob Dylan is making his own way across America, moving from city to city and I am due to cross paths with him in six days' time in Knoxville, TN. I don't know how much longer I can wait.

∽

Nashville is a city of music. You can drop in at any bar on Broadway here and hear a singer singing covers and taking requests or you can head up to Music Row and spot the headquarters of companies like Warner Music Group.

The real excitement on Music Row, though, comes from seeing RCA's Studios A and B where, among a host of other classic albums, Blonde on Blonde, John Wesley Harding and Nashville Skyline were brought into the world.

I'm underwhelmed by a lot of Nashville. Outside of Music Row and Broadway; once you've seen the Ryman Auditorium and the State Capital Building, there is not much to see apart from a seemingly never ending sprawl of tall, grey and lifeless buildings.

The museums are a saving grace, though and it's hard to be underwhelmed by the Country Music Hall of Fame. An impressive building looking out across the Walk of Fame Park and not far from where the Cumberland River cuts the city in two, there are generations of treasures locked away in the cabinets here. From the guitar that Jimmie Rodgers used to play to the pedal steel that rings in Lay, Lady, Lady; from Bob Wills' Fiddle to Taylor Swift's glittering rhinestone acoustic guitar, there is something for any music fan within these walls.

There is a fascinating exhibit on tracking the careers and collaborations of the legendary Gram Parsons and Emmylou Harris, complete with beautiful dresses, nudie suits, guitars, infographics and projections.

Whether it's seeing Jimmie Rodgers' guitar here or James Jamerson's bass in a cabinet down the road at the Musician's Hall of Fame, or the piano that Charlie Rich played on such all-time classics as Behind Closed Doors or The Most Beautiful Girl in the World, I can't help but feel like these instruments are wasting away. There's so much history locked away behind the glass but instruments are made to be played and I wonder what new songs are trapped inside them that we aren't hearing.

There's a Johnny Cash Museum in town, too, which is an obvious stop to make. Inside are some of the iconic black suits he wore on stage and during his hit TV show as the late sixties became the early seventies. They are colossal. I'm blown away by what a giant of a man he must have been. Maybe that's why he towered over popular music and popular culture for so long. Maybe that's why upon first meeting him, Bob Dylan walked around Cash, taking him in, before describing him as being akin to a great Oak tree.

I've stopped into the neon-clad Bourbon Street Blues Bar to try Dylan's new whiskey range, Heaven's Door. I've never enjoyed whiskey before but this has Bob Dylan's name on the label, some of his ironwork on the bottle and I *am* in Nashville so it would be rude not to at least try it.

I don't know anything about what I'm ordering so plum for the Double-Barrelled Whiskey, purely because I like the name. It's so harsh that I chase every sip with a grimace.

While I'm sat at the bar not enjoying my whiskey, I look back on the last two days and feel like I've seen everything in Nashville that I wanted to see already. I still have a few days here until I'm due to head to Knoxville. I have a look at Dylan's tour schedule and see another Tennessee date, tomorrow night. It takes a little while to find a ticket online for the sold out show, but by the time the ice in my drink has melted I've managed to get hold of one and booked a Greyhound and hostel, too.

I'm not sure whether it's the impulsive booking of another Bob Dylan show or the ice melting and taking the edge off the harshness of my drink, but it's a lot more palatable now and I lean back into my outdoor booth and look out across the night.

The whiskey makes it sweeter.

∞

The impulsive Greyhound ride from Nashville to Chattanooga turns out to be a magical journey. We drive past tranquil lakes and streams. An eagle swoops up and into the distant mountains and we kick the dust up of one of the longest roads I've ever travelled down into the green grass of the widest panoramic view I've ever seen.

Everything here is enormous. There is nothing but nature as far as the eye can see. It wasn't two hours since I was sat in the middle of the grey, cloudy sprawl of Nashville and yet here out in the middle of nowhere, the skies are blue and there is not a building in sight.

Beyond the horizon are endless mountains, trees and rivers. I wonder what the wildlife is like that we're rattling past; how many rabbits are burrowing in these pastures of plenty? How many black bears are roaming this land? Will we pass any elk or cougars or will the solitary eagle overhead be the only animal I see?

The journey is not long but when all that is ahead of you, and indeed beside and behind you, is the green expanse of open land it feels like it will last forever.

The Greyhound, incidentally, started out as a small shuttle bus service in Hibbing, Minnesota in 1914. Thirty-three years later, Beatty and Abraham Zimmerman would move to the town to raise their children, Robert and David. I wonder who has clocked up more miles on American soil in the years since; Greyhound Lines, Inc or Bob Dylan.

We drift on through the rolling fields, the lakes nearer to us now and the mountains further away. As we get closer to our destination, small and run-down buildings start to populate the landscape more and more. As we begin to twist through the narrowing roads we begin to pass small shacks and wooden houses. Some have their windows boarded up now that no one remains while some have a single rocking chair on the porch and cobwebs in the awnings.

The bus comes to a stop some way outside Chattanooga so I have to wait for a cab to take me into town proper. The driver tells me he doesn't hear accents like mine too much out here and asks what brings me to this little corner of the country. I'm here to see Bob Dylan, I tell him. "Oh", he says and drives me to my destination in silence. Perhaps he's a Donovan fan.

I pay my fare, thank the driver and head down Broad Street until I hit the Tennessee Rebel River. At the bank, there is an inflatable jetty that I teeter along to get as close to the calming water's air as possible. A small white dog runs past and launches itself into the river before paddling back to shore.

Down here in the South, there's Civil War in the air and the blood of the country's indigenous people in the soil.

Walking along the river, I stop at the murals and information boards describing events that took place here. Here being Ross's Landing, the place where the remaining Cherokee were driven out of their homes in 1838 on the Trail of Tears.

I stop and think a while about why any group of people should be displaced from their homes by colonialists in the pursuit of gold and about all the Natives who never made it to new land. I think about the similar crimes my own country has committed throughout history. I think about how, even almost two-hundred years later, the country I'm in and the country I'm from are still doing the exact same thing on an international scale.

I head back into town and get caught waiting at a crossing. An elderly couple, both clad in beige shorts and pastel coloured short sleeve tops, sandals and hats say hello. I'm not used to being approached on the street for a chat but they have warmth in their eyes and a smile on their lips as they're looking up at me.

I say hello back and they clock my foreign accent and the man is off. "Oh! You're from England? I've been to England a while back. I'm sure we caught you off guard, there! No one in England is very friendly, are they?" he says, a thick southern drawl drawing his words out. I tell him that while people back home are on the most part friendly enough, it's not often that we get talking to people we don't know on the streets. It doesn't stop him, "I remember being in London, it must have been thirty years ago. You try and talk to anyone on the tube there and they'll move away from you!" I'll have to remember that tactic next time I want a seat on the way home from work. "Say, don't you get scared with all that violence in London? We don't get any of that here, but when I was in England I was worried I was going to get shot."

I don't have it in me to remind this kind-faced, friendly old man which country we're talking about and which one we're in.

On Market Street I stop by to see the Chattanooga Choo-Choo. I only know it from The Andrews Sisters song but the train's arrival in 1850 was instrumental in building up the surrounding area into a commercial hub; the train connected the North and the South ("The place where corn meets cotton", as the saying went) and was a major asset during the Civil War when moving soldiers, munitions and provisions.

My final stop before heading to the theatre is to drop my bags off at The Crash Pad hostel, the cheapest place I could find to stay here on such short notice.

There are two men sat behind the reception area who greet me and check my details. They let me know that it's pretty quiet tonight and that I'm the only guest so I have the place to myself. After they ask what brings me to Chattanooga and I tell them Bob Dylan. They can't believe that he's in town and tell me they would love to be seeing him but had no idea he was playing here, there hasn't been any local advertising or any announcements.

Thinking about what they've said as I head to my bed, it strikes me that I haven't seen any signs or posters around the town all day advertising tonight's show. When I've seen Dylan in Europe there have been flyers, newspaper articles, spots on local radio and a general buzz in the air that he is coming. I wonder whether the excitement for Dylan stretches further in Europe, for whatever reason, or if it is a conscious decision by his promoters.

Despite the lack of advertisement, the line at the Tivoli Theatre stretches all the way down Broad Street when I get there. The marquee out the front is lit up with bright colours announcing the venue and the night's performer. It is magical, and the excitement at this impulsive bonus gig is really ramping up within my stomach.

Inside, the Tivoli Theatre is a stunning room and an intimate theatre, the perfect setting to witness Dylan's current style and performance.

By now, I know the show opens with Things Have Changed and it duly does, right on time. Dylan is at the baby grand, facing across the stage rather than out towards the crowd. His shining gold blazer is glittering and sparkling under the lights. He's approaching his eightieth year but is still as flamboyant as ever.

I try not to listen to recordings of shows in between attending concerts so that when I go, any changes in the setlist are a surprise and any new arrangements are fresh to my ears.

When I'm expecting Dylan to head centre stage to sing a Songbook tune and he instead stays at the piano to launch into a slow, lilting version of When I Paint My Masterpiece

I edge forward in my seat. The room is small, but the rendition makes it feel even smaller. I've never heard this song live before and the opening line and every uttering of the titular phrase draws a cheer from the audience.

Dylan's voice is quiet, commanding and powerful. The words are different now. He's singing about dodging lions still, but now they're fixing him with a mean and hungry look. While he can still hardly stand to see the mighty kings of the jungle, now that he has more years and experience behind him he can read their faces like a book.

Someday, he tells us, everything is going to be beautiful and the band quietly kicks in behind him. It's a powerful moment, and the power only grows when he starts blowing his harmonica. Bob Dylan has painted his masterpiece for us time and time again, and he is continuing to do so night after night.

The Standards have now all been entirely jettisoned from the setlist, replaced with all Dylan originals and classics such as Cry a While, Honest With Me, Make You Feel My Love and Scarlet Town; with the latter seeing Dylan striking Elvis Presley-esque poses between lines, including a grand finale where he reaches out to the crowd with one hand, the other holding his microphone stand at such an angle that it's practically horizontal in his grip.

There is another surprise to come when the band noodle around, practically freeform as if this is not a song at all and they're waiting for Dylan to decide what he wants to do next. They snap straight into place as he utters his most famous opening line; once upon a time you dressed so fine, threw the bums a dime, in your prime…

I haven't heard him play Like a Rolling Stone in six years.

Back then, in Philadelphia, it was an organ-led, muddy growling number. Tonight it is virtually unrecognisable, either from that performance or from any other. The verses pass by with Dylan's staccato, bullet-like singing until the pre-chorus descends back into freeform chaos, "how does it feel?" being dragged over numerous imploring bars.

A crash of the snare from George Receli and the band lock back in once again to the delight of the audience and a singalong breaks out as the melody now resembles what we all know as Like a Rolling Stone.

Early Roman Kings comes and goes, Stu Kimball trading in his guitar for a couple of handfuls of barely audible maracas, and then…

…and then, the most show stopping moment of the night. If When I Paint My Masterpiece was a treat, Like a Rolling Stone a surprise, what came next was unforgettable.

Again at the piano, again opening slowly, Dylan starts playing in the dark. The spotlight comes up at a low level, focusing on Dylan and none of the other band members on stage. He's expertly plucking a melody from the keys while Tony, Charlie and Stu take their hands off their instruments and a step back. George and Donnie have leaned back in their chairs and are watching Dylan as intently as I am.

He starts to sing a slow, lamenting and stunning version of Don't Think Twice, It's Alright – solo at the piano. Dylan hasn't played solo on stage in twenty years. He has somehow found a way to make this intimate venue even more intimate, still.

His voice is haunting. It's drenched in heartbreak, regret, remorse, experience and acceptance. It is the single most moving performance I have ever seen.

Four years ago, when I last saw him perform this song, it was an up-tempo country waltz. Now it is a shattering, mournful and devastating ode.

It is testament to the underrated musical ability of Bob Dylan that he can find all the different versions within these songs.

And it isn't just tempos, styles and lyrics that he changes, either. He switches up the keys he plays in as regularly as the other components and has the ability to transpose songs into new keys on the spot.

When it was first recorded in 1962, Dylan played Don't Think Twice solo on the acoustic guitar – his fingerpicking accompaniment was so beyond the level of his perceived musical ability that biographer Clinton Heylin has wasted a lot of breath and ink trying to prove that it was Bruce Langhorne, not Dylan, playing the guitar on the recording. It wasn't. New recordings from various locations that year have proven that, unless Langhorne happened to be at every party Dylan was taped at playing the song in 1962, Dylan was the guitarist on the track, all along.

Fifty-six years later and we are being treated to a new solo version, this time with an expansive piano part rising and falling under Dylan's sustained vocals. The song feels like it has racked up a lifetime of loss and regret in the time that it has grown up, too, and Dylan wrings out every last drop by the time his harmonica flourish sees it out. No one is left in their seat at song's end as a standing ovation rightly breaks out.

There is a lot of commentary online that since Dylan started singing the Songbook tracks his voice has improved and he is singing a lot better. While it's hard to argue that his vocals are getting stronger with each passing year, culminating with these new versions of such classic songs, to say it is a result of working his way through the Great American Songbook is to ignore the quality of his singing in 2013 on Forgetful Heart and What Good Am I?, in 2014 on Girl From the North Country and on Shelter From the Storm. The reason Bob Dylan sang the Great American Songbook songs so well is because *he is a good singer.* He is not a good singer *because he sang the Great American Songbook songs.*

The song is hanging in the air and in my mind all through Love Sick and it's only during the wild ride of Thunder on the Mountain that I'm brought back into the room.

By the time that Dylan runs to centre stage to bow and throw his arms out wide at the end of Gotta Serve Somebody, my giddiness and excitement has worked its way back up to how I felt leaving the London Palladium last year or leaving the Hammersmith Apollo in 2011 and I feel emotional at getting to share all these experiences with the greatest songwriter and performer of our lifetimes.

∞

On Halloween morning I walk into Knoxville's Old City, crossing the long Gay Street Bridge, and with it the Tennessee River.

I arrived last night at the same time as the moon did and had to take the long walk from the bus terminal to my Airbnb under the cover of darkness.

The road shifted under my feet and became an unmade gravel path, the houses on either side turned to trees.

Engulfed by the pitch black night and hearing only the crunch of the gravel under my shoes and the rustle of the trees, I felt even further away from home than I really am. When I made it to my accommodation and the door swung open to reveal the friendly giant who was hosting me for the night, it was a huge relief to get inside and see a welcoming face.

It's 9 am but already everywhere I go I am passing people in costume; painted faces, masks and spooky costumes around every corner. I step into a small café for a vegan breakfast and there are ghouls and witches at every table.

Afterwards, I head up to the Tennessee Theatre to scope out the venue for the night and see that Dylan's huge, obsidian black Mercedes "Beat the Street" tour bus is already parked out back.

From there I head up to the observation deck of Knoxville's Sunsphere and take in the view across the city and beyond to the Great Smoky Mountains.

After getting an overview of the city from above, I stop by at the East Tennessee Historical Society to get a deeper look into the region's past. Inside are over 13,000 artefacts from Native American tools and weapons to Civil War guns and cannons; there are household items from pioneer and settler times and there are clothes that the people who lived on this land two hundred years ago would have worn. There is a canoe that the Natives would have used to traverse the Tennessee River and there are carts that the settlers would have used to roam the land.

Walking into this museum with its Old West artefacts and modelled stores and bedrooms from the era is like walking into the world that "Love and Theft" and Modern

Times come from. That for the latter Dylan lifted several lines from Civil War poet Henry Timrod makes the album feel even more era appropriate.

My final stop before joining the queue at the theatre is Merchants of Beer in the heart of the Old City. I sit at the bar and order a Heaven's Door, this time the Tennessee Bourbon. It's so much smoother than the Double-Barrell Whiskey and it warms your mouth with each sip.

After a couple more glasses, it's time to head Downtown for the show.

Earlier on in the day the streets were filled with people in Halloween costume but tonight, anyone who is dressed up is dressed up as Bob Dylan. It's like walking onto the set of I'm Not There.

Curly hair wigs and harmonica holders, dark sunglasses, polkadots and moonbeams are all around me. When the real Dylan takes to the stage at 8 pm sharp, he has his Bob Dylan mask on and masquerades his way through Things Have Changed.

With its 1,600 capacity, this is the smallest venue I've ever seen him in but when you're in a room with a giant such as Bob Dylan, even the biggest venues begin to feel intimate anyway.

The show three days ago in Chattanooga was full of surprises for me because I wasn't expecting a lot of the songs and even less prepared for the arrangements. I should know what's coming next tonight, how I'm going to feel with each passing song but the memory of the show before has deserted me while this one is taking place and every passing moment is as fresh, vibrant and gripping as the last.

When I Paint My Masterpiece is just as jaw-dropping when you're expecting it, the harmonica solo in Make You Feel My Love is just as gut-wrenching and Don't Think Twice, It's Alright is still just as heart-stopping as it was the first time around.

Tonight I am sat about ten rows from the front of the stage, on the right hand side of the arena, directly in front of Dylan at the piano. When he heads centre stage for Scarlet Town – its haunting, ghostly banjo-led arrangement making it the perfect Halloween performance – I have a clear and close up view of Dylan's new moves.

He grabs the mic stand and drapes it across his hip like a gunslinger. He bends at the knee and throws out a hand at the end of each line like he's tossing the words away to make room for what's coming next.

By the song's end he has covered every inch of centre stage and finds himself facing side on, but slowly twists round and stretches his arm out towards the crowd again. Don't reach out for us, we say, can't you see we're drowning too?

The biggest fright of the night is when a fan scrambles up on to the stage during All Along the Watchtower (the only change from the Chattanooga concert, replacing Ballad of a Thin Man in the setlist) and throws his arms around Dylan from behind.

The room collectively holds its breath to wait and see what is going on. The music from the stage fizzles into an echo. Dylan simply turns, nods at the stage intruder and then walks away while security grab him and drag him from the stage. Nothing can phase Bob Dylan anymore. At 78, he's already seen it all.

By the end of the year I have added a Paul McCartney concert to my roll-call of gigs this year. He even brought Ringo out during the encore, which means I have seen Bob Dylan, The Rolling Stones and the surviving members of The Beatles in performance this year.

A friend quips to me that they bet I wish it was 1966 and I was seeing them all then.

I don't. The fact that these performers are still with us, that they're still working and that they're still singing their songs for us is something that I wouldn't change for the world.

CHAPTER EIGHT

THE TIMES WE'VE KNOWN

Grand Rex. Paris, France. April 11, 2019
Grand Rex. Paris, France. April 13, 2019
Hyde Park. London, England. July 12, 2019

Following Bob Dylan on the road has allowed me to see a whole world of incredible sights. I've looked down over New York City from the top of the Empire State Building and seen the Colosseum in Rome; the works of Gaudi dotted around Barcelona and a 400 year old shipwreck in Stockholm's Vasa Museum; the Appalachian Mountain range that bore so much great music in a far off mystical time and in 2019 his trail led me to the Eiffel Tower, to the Louvre and Mona Lisa, Venus de Milo and the portrait of Julienne and Gabrielle d'Estrées as well as to the Notre Dame, one day before it burnt down. Incidentally, it has brought me closer to events like this than I would have preferred on more than one occasion; a day after returning from Stockholm in 2017, a terrorist drove a car down the Drottninggatan and the same happened on La Ramblas in

Barcelona a day after I returned to London the next year. So it goes.

∽

If I've seen a lot of incredible things and brought the stories home with me, they're nothing on the collection of tales Bob Dylan has to tell about every major city he has performed in throughout his life.

Playing a concert in Paris on his twenty-fifth birthday in 1966 he took to the stage with an antagonistically large United States flag draped across the back of the stage. He seemed to be playfully combative with the crowd, perhaps in response to the audiences he'd faced everywhere so far that year who had been down right combative with him – the Manchester crowd who he performed to a few days prior famously re-christening him as 'Judas' for having the temerity to play an electric guitar onstage – but the crowd at L'Olympia seemed to be more in on the joke as he slurs a few attempted lines in French and spends a lifetime tuning his acoustic guitar before delivering the goods when it really matters.

Thirty-six years later on stage at Paris' Zénith Arena, on one of the handful of songs that were still in his setlist from that 1966 world tour, Desolation Row, Dylan makes a special effort to correctly pronounce "Notre Dame". The appreciative screams, cheers and cries from the audience cover up the fact that the following line now no longer rhymes, but it doesn't matter, it's a lovely moment and one of those nods to his location and audience that is more special than a simple "Hello, Paris!" could ever be.

Indeed, getting a "Hello, how are we all doing tonight?" might even be less likely than getting a live performance of Ballad in Plain D at this point and some sections of the fanbase seem to take issue with this. Casual fans, too, will frequently tell you about the times they saw Dylan and he didn't even say hello to the crowd once. Evidently, his lyrics are not enough for some.

A few years later before another gig in Paris, Dylan phones Lenny Kravitz up and invites himself over to his place before later suggesting they head out for a walk around town together, despite the pouring rain. Anyone who tried to tell a friend they'd passed Bob Dylan and Lenny Kravitz sat on a bench getting drenched in the Jardin du Luxembourg would surely have raised a few eyebrows or an encore of "je ne te crois pas, tu es un menteur!"

∞

In 1961 Dylan played his first headline show, performing a tight seven song setlist at New York's Carnegie Hall. A few years later and he was in the audience at the same venue to see France's most legendary songwriter and performer, Charles Aznavour; a concert that evidently made an impression – when asked by Kurt Loader in a 1987 interview for Rolling Stone who the best live performer he has seen is, Dylan mentions that concert at Carnegie Hall, saying that seeing Aznavour "blew his brains out".

In 1998 they were both performing in New York – Aznavour with a three week residency at the Marquis Theatre on Broadway and Dylan only passing through on his Never Ending Tour.

After finishing the tenth song of his Madison Square Garden concert, that night at Carnegie Hall is obviously on Dylan's mind again as he steps up to the microphone and mumbles, "I'm going to try something here" and the crowd hushes. On certain tours, Dylan is chattier than others but as he gets older he seems to speak less and less, so that now whenever he decides to talk between songs the crowd usually listens; "There's a guy playing up the street that I've always liked, Charles Aznavour's his name. I guess he's from someplace in France. Anyway, I saw him 'round here a long time ago and he's playing up there, now, so I'll try and play one of his songs." He takes a long pause before adding, seemingly to himself "I usually play these things all to myself, but, I feel like I'm all by myself now anyway."

He launches in to a spellbinding and moving version of The Times We've Known, originally in French as Les Bon Moments when sung by Aznavour. It's a hushed performance, giving the song the reverence it deserves and carries a power on the translated lyrics.

Eleven years later on stage at the Palais des Congrès de Paris Dylan covered the song again. Forty-five years on from the Carnegie Hall show and this time it's Aznavour who is in the crowd to see Dylan. This time there is no introduction, he lets the lyrics speak for themselves. His voice is weathered and the performance is not as moving as it had been a decade earlier but the strength of the words still shine through.

∞

Ten years on again and I am in Paris to see Bob Dylan at the Grand Rex. Last year I was hoping to see Charles Aznavour at the Royal Albert Hall in London but as he was 94 I'd left it too late. The concert never happened and later in the year he sadly died.

This is the first time Dylan is playing in Paris since that news broke so while it's not possible to see Charles Aznavour singing Les Bon Moments live, I am at least hoping to hear Dylan singing The Times We've Known.

Increasingly Dylan is bringing his show to ever more and more gorgeous rooms; whether it's the Gran Teatre del Liceu in Barcelona, the Tivoli in Chattanooga or here tonight in France at the Grand Rex.

Originally opening its doors in 1932 and modelled on Radio City Music Hall in New York, The Grand Rex is a converted movie theatre with a capacity of just under 3,000, an absolutely staggering number of seats for a cinema.

The marquee out the front looks like a casino now that it's lit up and the sky is growing dark. I'm here with my mum and we head indoors, through the crowd and along the red carpets up to the escalators and enter the auditorium. It is beautiful inside. We have a perfect, unobstructed view of the stage which is backed by a neon arch, lit up with reds and blues. Either side of it is a mock Greco-Roman style building, "overgrown" with plants and busts of unidentified nymphs, goddesses and muses like the bust of Athena who sits at the side of the stage, watching over Dylan's shoulder wherever he performs.

The ceiling has artificial stars that twinkle throughout the night. Sitting in this room is like sitting inside a dream.

"Sure, I dream," Dylan's character Jack Fate says in a particularly moving scene from 2003's weird and wonderful

Masked & Anonymous, "in my dreams I walk through fire with intense heat". Tonight, Bob Dylan and his Band are bringing the intense heat with them, right off the bat.

They open with an unrelenting Things Have Changed. It feels like the rest of the world is melting away with each line. He's played this at almost every concert of his I've been to and true to the titular phrase, it's been different every time, too. He can get so many variations out of the same chord progression, find so many ways inside a song and wring so many different meanings out of the same words that coming back night after night is always exciting.

∽

Some of those who have been following the Never Ending Tour for longer than I have, and indeed for longer than I've even been alive, lament the fact that in recent years starting at the tail end of 2013 the setlist has become more rigid in structure.

For most of the "NET", song selection varied quite widely from night to night – often a portion of the songs would stay the same and others would rotate in, some tracks would appear for a while and then never be heard of again and some would make a one off appearance and go on to become legendary for that reason.

Occasionally patterns would emerge and astute fans noticed that some songs would only be played on certain days of the week while on others, that same slot in the set would be filled with The Lonesome Death of Hattie Carroll or John Brown. Sometimes there was a variation on what would be played whether the show was indoors or outside.

By the end of 2011 and early 2012, most of the show was fixed with a handful of tracks that were wildcards each night but always ending with the same run of Greatest Hits.

The biggest shake up for a while came in this period when tracks from Tempest were finally eased into performances and the show started to focus more and more on Dylan's latter day material.

On the Autumn leg of the tour in 2013, starting in Oslo on October 10, what later became known amongst Dylan fans as "The Set" made its debut. Those who bemoan the fact that the songs rarely change night after night like they did in the good old days are forgetting that for most of Dylan's career he has stuck fairly rigidly to a small pool of songs on any given tour – ostensibly the same show was presented the world over on the legendary 1966 tour, Tour 74 regularly featured the same songs on consecutive nights, as did shows on other such major tours as the Rolling Thunder Revue, 1978's unique and underappreciated outing, the astounding Gospel tours of 1979/80 and 1984's stadium tour of Europe.

Where Dylan's alchemy in performance lies is in singing a song you've heard a hundred times before in a way you never imagined it could be done. It doesn't matter if you hear him sing Beyond Here Lies Nothin' every night of the year; each time you hear it you're hearing that version for the first time.

Another thing that is overlooked in discussion about The Set is that it doesn't *really* exist. Bob Dylan is held to a different set of expectations by his fans than other artists seem to be; a lot of artists have static setlists that they take around the world without complaint to promote a new album or deluxe edition reissue. When Dylan does it, his fans have something to say about it.

A closer inspection of the songs he performs in concert from 2013 onwards reveals that there is still quite a lot of variation happening after all. That songs like It's Alright Ma (I'm Only Bleeding), Huck's Tune, Workingman's Blues #2 (complete with all new lyrics), Waiting For You, Most Likely You Go Your Way (And I'll Go Mine), Forgetful Heart, Girl From the North Country, To Ramona, Til I Fell in Love With You, Blind Willie McTell and Visions of Johanna; Dignity, Lenny Bruce, Million Miles, Tweedle Dee & Tweedle Dum, Not Dark Yet and Like a Rolling Stone, All Along the Watchtower, Ballad of a Thin Man, Jolene and I'll Be Your Baby Tonight – songs from every corner of his career – drift in and out of rotation shows that there is still a lot of mixing it up going on, not to mention the injection of Great American Songbook standards that join the show in 2015 *as well as* covers of songs such as Willie Nelson's Sad Songs & Waltzes, Tom Petty's Learning to Fly, James Brown's It's a Man's, Man's, Man's World and even an instrumental Free Bird (presumably upon request).

In 2014 there are ninety three different songs played across the year's tours, including ten one off performances and a further seventeen tracks that are played ten times or less. This pattern stays the same throughout the next five years but yet the myth of "The Set" persists, nonetheless.

∞

Dylan stays at the piano for 1964's classic It Ain't Me, Babe and there's a smattering of an audience singalong at the chorus' sardonically jubilant "no, no, no! It ain't *me* you're looking for". It most certainly *is* him I've come to France in search of and, as elusive as he can supposedly be, I feel lucky to find him right in front of me, now.

When I listen to Charles Aznavour it doesn't seem to matter that I can't speak French to understand what he's singing – beyond a smattering of phrases and words I've picked up to know well enough when he's singing about love, bohemia, ageing, regrets, time passing, a couple of guitars or drinking -, his essence and his tone, his phrasing and his timing and the honesty in his voice is what moves me.

Tonight in the stunning Grand Rex Theatre, Bob Dylan is leaving a similar impression on my mum. She leans in to me during the harmonica solo on Simple Twist of Fate and confesses that she isn't understanding every word he sings, but that it doesn't matter; the music and his singing are still so moving and so beautiful.

Indeed, Dylan has shown throughout his career an ability to move you without necessarily being comprehensible. For an artist famed for being so good with words, he has at times transcended the need for a finished lyric; proven by the unfinished 1966 song I Can't Leave Her Behind, the Basement Tape recording I'm Not There, the 1986 outtake To Fall in Love With You – each of which are incomplete lyrically but fully realised emotionally – and the first of three performances of The Grateful Dead's Black Muddy River in 1992, where Dylan doesn't let the fact he clearly doesn't know the words stop him delivering a devastating rendition.

The songs are the same tonight as when I saw him last Halloween, but since the first note all time outside this room has ceased to exist and I can't remember what comes next. If you asked me before the show what songs would be most likely to be played, I could have reeled off last night's setlist from memory but as I'm stunned and mesmerised once again by the music and presence, it's a pleasant surprise when Honest With Me becomes Trying to Get to Heaven, becomes Scarlet Town, becomes Make You Feel My Love – complete with a searing, breath-taking harmonica solo.

Cry a While has been transformed; no longer a fluctuating blues, now the band are essentially playing Link Wray's Rumble underneath Dylan's singing. It's a song he seems to have an affinity with, going so far to describe it as the greatest instrumental of all time and performing it live in concert in 2005, following Wray's death.

It's not even the first time Dylan has used it as the basis for one of his songs in concert, either. In 2010 he opened his performance at the Hop Farm Festival with Rainy Day Women #12 & #35, standing at the keyboard and playing its usual arrangement. After the third verse he wandered away from his keyboard to pick up his guitar and while the band continued to play Rainy Day Women, Dylan started thrashing out the chords to Rumble.

Such is the autonomy of his band, it takes them about two bars to follow him into the new path and transition into the new arrangement, mid-song. When Dylan launches into a guitar solo, the crowd erupts.

If I felt like time outside the room had come to a halt since the show began, Dylan stops time within the room, too, with that gorgeous arrangement of Don't Think Twice, It's

Alright. As we get to the final verse, the band ease their way into the song and join Dylan who is singing as if he is all by himself, now. I realise that I am holding my breath and can't remember for how long I've been doing so. Next to me, tears are rolling down my mum's cheek and I am almost certain that elsewhere in the theatre everyone else must be having a similar reaction to us.

Two songs later and Dylan and His Band have traded in the sentimental for the raucous, the tear jerking for the hair raising. Thunder on the Mountain has become a different beast from the setlist padding it used to be and Dylan spits the words out like his life is depending on it. When you make touring and performing your whole raison d'être, perhaps it really does.

To close out the main show, we're treated to a funky, loose but driving Gotta Serve Somebody. This band really can play *anything*.

Dylan is lively, bouncing on his toes as he riffs with the lyrics and feels like he's finding rhymes on the spot before returning to the chorus.

Each year I see him he's livelier and more full of life than the last; indeed, he's become the physical embodiment of his own phrase "I was so much older then / I'm younger than that now" but it's still a surprise to see him almost run to centre stage from his piano once he's done singing his song and the band move into the final instrumental verse.

He strikes a few poses (hand on hip, finger guns, fists up like a boxer and then an open hand flourish that is just a few shakes short of jazz hands) and soaks up the adulation of the crowd and then heads off stage for a quick break before the encore.

He's just finished singing Blowin' in the Wind and a nasty, dirty, bluesy and beautiful It Takes a Lot to Laugh, It Takes a Train to Cry and heads back to centre stage for more posing, more cheers and whistles from the crowd and, it seems, more music.

The lights have gone down but there is still noise coming from the stage and I realise I've taken a step forward in anticipation because I was expecting that to be the last song of the night.

Aside from the faux stars in the ceiling and a few phone screens held up to try and catch a snapshot before the chance slips away, it is pitch black in the room but here comes the opening riff of Just Like Tom Thumb's Blues.

The lights come back up as the song kicks into gear but Dylan is nowhere to be seen. Donnie Herron is playing a melody on his lap-steel in a tone that is so unlike anything he's played while sitting behind Dylan all night or in any of the years I've seen him. It's Santo & Johnny in overdrive. He gets up, bows and with a cheer from the crowd, takes his leave from the stage.

Charlie Sexton takes centre stage with a soulful guitar line that is full of flourishes which are part Eddie Hinton and part border-town romance. The crowd by now are clapping along in time with the beat that George Receli has locked into on the drums and the guitar solo continues until there are no more beautiful notes for Charlie Sexton left to play. He bows and leaves the stage to Tony Garnier and George Receli.

Tony Garnier is a crowd favourite and his bass solo is drawing whoops and cheers from all around me until he, too, puts down his instrument and takes his leave. Receli is the last man standing, now, and expands upon the short drum solo from Thunder on the Mountain, before abruptly stopping, tossing his sticks over his shoulder, standing and heading off stage and into the night.

∞

Over the course of the week in Paris we've done a lot of walking and taken in a lot of sights and history.

We've been to the Muséum national d'histoire naturelle and walked with dinosaurs like Diplodocus, Allosaurus and Triceratops. We've been to the Louvre and seen a host of classical characters from Ancient Greece, immortalised in marble and stone as well as Renaissance works including Mona Lisa with her highway blues. We've seen the Sacré-Cœur Basilica, the Place de la Bastille and the Arc de Triomphe; we've walked the Champs-Élysées, seen the Eiffel Tower, the Moulin Rouge and we're among the last people to gaze up at Notre Dame before it's reduced in parts to ash. I've wandered up to the Catacombs of Paris and through the Montparnasse Cemetery. We've walked the banks of the Seine, flicked through books in Shakespeare and Company and I've picked up some Django Reinhardt, Jacques Brel and Muddy Waters discs in a small record shop near the Arènes de Lutèce.

As I settle in to my seat to spend another evening with Bob Dylan and His Band it strikes me that on this trip to Paris we have had a tour of all history – pre, ancient and recent. It feels appropriate to conclude a trip such as that with another night with the most historically important artist of our times; with someone who carries all that history within him and lets you know and hear it.

Bob Dylan, perhaps, is as culturally significant and important as anything else we've seen in this city during the week.

It's July 12 and I'm supposed to be taking a seat at the back of the Hammersmith Apollo with my best buddy to watch Jerry Seinfeld perform his latest stand up show.

Where I'm supposed to be and where I am, though, are two different things. As soon the British Summer Time festival announced that this year's main event would be taking place on July 12 and would be headlined by Neil Young and Bob Dylan, I text my friend to let him know I couldn't make it to the Seinfeld show.

There's a lot of build up today. It's all my friends and I have been talking about for weeks. My friend Dan will be in the crowd with one of his pals. It's his first Dylan show, while his friend is there to see Neil Young. All of the online Dylan community who live in the UK will be here today and I'm sure we'll all cross paths, knowingly or not, throughout the course of the festival.

On the day, the build-up begins sitting on the grass in the sunshine just the other side of the festival site's perimeter. There are maybe fifty people in front of us in the queue which should allow for a decent spot, considering around sixty-five thousand will be turning up throughout the day. Once the gates open and we make our way inside, we find that it doesn't matter how early we've got in; there is a fenced off area that stops us from getting too close to the stage and so we head for a ticket office to upgrade our view and are let into the inner circle.

I've been to a few of these festivals, now – to see The Strokes in 2015 for one of the more memorable gigs of my life, to see Carole King perform Tapestry in its entirety a year later for a magical day, and to see Green Day in 2017 – but I've never been as excited to see anyone here as this.

The excitement for today's show began ramping up long before we got to Hyde Park, though.

Two weeks after we got home from Paris, Rolling Thunder Revue: A Bob Dylan Story By Martin Scorsese was announced. I booked half the day off work for the day of its release so I could stay home and watch it as soon as I woke up, and then we got tickets to see it at the Prince Charles Theatre off Leicester Square.

The first time I watched the film I loved it, the second time I rolled my eyes at the deceptions and make believe but watching it on a big screen in the cinema was where the film came alive and the suspension of reality was the most natural and where the joke landed best.

I'd seen a 24 year old Bob Dylan in D.A Pennebaker's seminal Don't Look Back in the cinema at London's BFI Southbank a few years before, but to get to see and hear 78 year old Bob Dylan on the big screen, knowing we were about to see 78 year old Bob Dylan on stage in less than a month, was a wonderful and exciting moment.

Back in Hyde Park and the first of the day's performers hits the stage. The occasion obviously didn't escape Sam Fender as he tells the crowd what a surreal moment it is to open for Bob Dylan. He tells us it's a moment that he'll tell his grandkids about and to be honest, if I was on the same stage that Bob Dylan was about to sing from I wouldn't wait until I had grandkids to tell the tale.

He plays a short set full of highlights, including Will We Talk and Hypersonic Missiles. Next up is Cat Power whose performance includes a cover of the traditional 'He Was a Friend of Mine', sung by a young Bob Dylan in 1962, as well as one especially for Dylan, 2008's "Song to Bobby".

Laura Marling holds the growing crowd in the palm of her hand as she works her way through ten songs, starting with the incredible Master Hunter, complete with Dylan reference to close out the second verse, as she drawls 'if you want a woman who can call your name, it ain't me babe / No, no, no, it ain't me babe". If anyone in the crowd was unfamiliar with her work, she will have instantly won them over with the reference.

Neil Young takes to the stage at around 6 pm. We've been on our feet for about seven hours now but despite the great music on show before this, to me, it feels like the day is about to begin.

He kicks off his show with Mansion on the Hill. I'm not that familiar with Neil Young's music beyond the classics like Harvest Moon or The Needle and the Damage Done.

The day's music has been wonderful, each performer putting on a great show and delivering such consistently good music, but from the first note that Neil Young + The Promise of the Real play it is clear that a heavyweight has arrived and the 65,000 strong audience collectively takes a step forward to get closer to the action. I'm drawn into Mansion on the Hill, its harmonies fleshing out in my mind the images that Young is singing about.

He barrels straight into another song I don't know but immediately love, Over and Over, and it isn't until the ninth song that he plays one I recognise, the beautiful and mesmerising Heart of Gold.

In 2002, Bob Dylan had been including a lot of covers in his setlists; old Appalachian ballads with their roots going back to English or Scottish folk songs as well as some written by his contemporaries and peers like The Rolling Stones (Brown Sugar), Warren Zevon (Lawyers, Guns and Money, Accidentally Like a Martyr, Mutineer) and Neil Young. He performed Old Man thirty three times between the start of October and end of November that year and it's a treat to hear the song sung by its writer, now, knowing Dylan will be following him onstage shortly.

Young closes out his set with Rockin' in the Free World. I text Dan asking how many false endings he reckons there will be.

The song seems to wind down and finish once; a cacophony of guitars and overdrive fuzz, then a snare hit and we're straight back into the chorus. Twice and then that snare hits again. The crowd don't miss a beat and joins Neil Young for another go round on the chorus with as much force and joy as at any other point in the song's expansive eight minutes. The drum hits again but this time there's no room to singalong as the band draw out a final, grungy note and instead of singing, Young screams into the mic to Keep on Rockin' in the Free World and the song is over.

He returns for an encore and I don't know any of these songs. I haven't known many of the seventeen songs so far but it hasn't impeded the enjoyment of his performance at all. He's vacillated between gentle acoustic arrangements and aggressive, grungy punk throughout the set and given us a tour of a musical landscape unlike anything else we've heard today. I've fallen in love with some of the songs I've heard for the first time and forgotten some of the rest but overall it has been a thoroughly enjoyable, ramshackle and raucous performance. What a way to be introduced to some of these songs; in the blistering sun shining down on London's Hyde Park, surrounded by music fans of all ages.

The band kicks in for one last song before splitting and I feel like Young is making a statement with the song choice, but the delivery of the message is more comical than convincing. Whatever *it* is that he's blasting as a "Piece of Crap" with each passing line, the title phrase feels a more appropriate description of whatever this song is supposed to be.

Considering the tracks he has in his catalogue to pick from, considering the songs he *didn't* sing, Piece of Crap is a weird way to go out. It'd be like seeing Dylan live and he closes out a barnstorming show with Wiggle Wiggle.

∞

Dylan's piano is being rolled onto the stage, a double bass is brought out for Tony Garnier and the mics are being tested.

The air is warm and abuzz with people talking about what they've just heard and what is still to come. Every now and again someone pushes past us with an armful of beers, evidently not wanting to be caught short during the final set of the night or wanting to leave their post.

A man behind us has sat down and pulled a folder out of his bag and is rifling through reams of paper; the setlists from every previous show this year are printed out and bound together, the lyrics for each song ordered and ready to be followed along if and when the time comes later.

A woman behind me asks her daughter who the statue is on Dylan's piano and what it means. I can hear the "I don't know" response and so I tell her it's Athena, the Goddess of Wisdom and the Arts. "But what does it *mean*?" she wants to know. Sometimes it's not enough to know what things mean, sometimes you have to know what things don't mean, as well.

As I continue to look around the crowd behind me, going beyond the horizon as far as I can tell, being bathed in an orange light of the setting sun, I'm struck by the enormity of this crowd.

The 65,000 strong gathering is probably as many people as have been combined at all twenty-one previous Dylan gigs I've been to, if not more.

The size of this crowd is testament to the drawing power of an artist who began his career in a small club in New York 59 years ago; to the amount of lives he has touched in that time and to how enduring and timeless his work is.

Standing here side by side with my mum; who was there on the first night in Hammersmith with me, who was there with me in Philadelphia the first time I left the country to see him, who was in Paris with me earlier in the year, who put up with years of my thrashing out new Dylan covers on my guitar in my bedroom or listened while I spoke about him at length at any given opportunity, and who was by my side the night all three of us exchanged eye contact in the Royal Albert Hall back in another lifetime, is a memory I will cherish forever.

I turn back to the stage as a roar whips up and the band file into the spotlight, followed onto the stage by a man whose presence alone somehow outweighs that of all the 65,000 people gathered here in the midsummer sun to watch him.

Dylan spent the day making an impromptu trip to London's Halcyon Gallery; his last minute arrival causing the gallery to be closed to the public for a short time and most of the staff given time for a break while he wandered around to see how his work was being presented.

In Hyde Park, he is fully in charge; fully engaged and fully in command of the presentation of his work. He is in the highest spirits as he dances and smiles his way through his headline set. Just like the 65,000 of us in the audience do.

CHAPTER NINE

CAN'T GO TO PARADISE NO MORE

Today I wake up at about 6 am. Ever since lockdown began my sleeping pattern has been all over the place. It could be worse; all around the world, people are dying prematurely from a combination of the deadly Covid-19 pandemic and horrendous government mismanagement of the situation.

True, we're in unprecedented times but these feel like the worst possible times to have the likes of Donald Trump, Boris Johnson and Jair Bolsonaro at the helm.

Since my work shut its office doors on March 12 I've been at home every day. The night before that I'd been at the Royal Albert Hall watching Bryan Ferry; seizing the chance to squeeze one final gig in when a colleague offered me their ticket as they were, fairly, too scared to be in a crowd of that size anymore.

For the last two weeks I've been working remotely; watching movies online with friends and digitalising what had until now been real-life interactions, taking the extra hours to cook better meals and to play more guitar; adjusting fairly quickly to the new isolated world.

I had tickets to watch Southampton take on Norwich at Carrow Road and tickets to see Randy Newman at the London Palladium in Summer. Neither event will be going ahead, now.

I'd been intending to fly to Japan to see Bob Dylan and His Band this year, too. His performances coincided with the Cherry Blossom season and the flights had been fairly reasonably priced. Judging by recordings, his shows in the country are always special; whether he was playing the Nippon Budokan in Tokyo in 1978, at The Great Music Experience in Nara in 1994 – backed by a full orchestra – or, most recently, at the Fuji Rock Festival in 2018.

I'd also intended to fly to America to see his joint tour with Nathaniel Rateliff and the Night Sweats and Hot Club of Cowtown; most likely in Bethel Woods so that I had an excuse to explore the nearby town of Woodstock with all its obvious Dylan history. Of course, those things won't be happening this year either. We can't go to Paradise no more, too many people have been killed back there.

I rub my eyes and check my phone. A goodnight message that I'd fallen asleep before receiving is the only notification I have so I reply and open Twitter to see what horrible things have happened outside the house in the eight hours I've been sleeping.

"Greetings to my fans and followers with gratitude for all your support and loyalty across the years." There is a tweet, of all things, from Bob Dylan, of all people. "This is an unreleased song we recorded a while back that you might find interesting. Stay safe, stay observant and may God be with you. Bob Dylan"

I sit upright, put my glasses on and pause for a moment to make sure that I know it's real and not a dream. A new Bob Dylan song. A Bob Dylan song that I'm about to hear for the very first time.

I click the link, lie back down and close my eyes as the song starts, the piano cascading gently before he starts talk-singing. It goes on and it goes on and it goes on. Seventeen minutes pass before I open my eyes again. Light is starting to creep in through my window between a crack in the curtain. I receive a good morning message but dismiss the notification immediately to scroll the song back to the start and listen to it right straight through three more times in a row.

Maybe this year is not going to be all bad, after all.

∞

On February 1, I saw the final performance of Girl From the North Country at the Gielgud Theatre. I'd first seen the show during its original run in town, with my Nan in early 2018 when it was still at the Noel Coward Theatre and had the original cast, including towering performances from Ciarán Hinds and Shirley Henderson.

Both performances remain some of my favourite Bob Dylan days out in all my ten years of travelling with him, and yet he was nowhere to be seen on either occasion; his presence hanging heavy over the room and yet remaining out of sight and out of reach each time.

It's nice to know, looking back, that even if I don't get to see Bob Dylan live this year, I've still at least seen and heard his music alive in performance once.

Set in Duluth, Minnesota in 1934, the musical tells the story of the intersecting lives of a family who run a guesthouse and the guests who are passing through. The performances and arrangement of nineteen Bob Dylan songs go to show the timeless nature of his writing, the universality and the craftsmanship of the songs as well as the strength of the actors.

One performance, particularly, stands out above the rest First sung by Sheila Atim and more recently when played by Gloria Obianyo, Tight Connection To My Heart (Has Anyone Seen My Love?) is, without doubt, the highlight of the show and as haunting, moving and spirited a performance as you will see anywhere from The West End to Broadway.

It was enough to bring my Nan, despite not particularly being a Bob Dylan fan, to tears. The second time I see the show, this time with my mum for company, it has the same effect on me.

∞

Looking back over the last four months, I realise I've managed to fit a lot into the short window when it was possible to fit anything in.

As well as Girl From the North Country and Bryan Ferry, I'd seen The Growlers, Angel Olsen and Girl Ray, too and was pleased to have found the time to see the monumental Bong Joon-Ho film Parasite in the cinema.

Apparently Bob Dylan had been busy, as well, as three weeks after Murder Most Foul was released and climbed its way to #1 on the Digital Rock Charts – incredibly, his first Billboard #1 Single – he released another track, I Contain Multitudes. Another three weeks on, False Prophet was unleashed on the world alongside the announcement that Dylan's first new album of original material in eight years was on the way.

⁓

As is always the case when Dylan takes a break from performing to release a record, a statement, a line of Whiskey or to appear in a car advert, the forensic analysis of False Prophet started up before anyone could get through the song's whole six minutes.

Murder Most Foul and I Contain Multitudes were littered with explicit cultural references; Bud Powell and Anne Frank, Wolfman Jack and Beethoven.

False Prophet is just as densely packed with references, but they're more hidden than on the first two singles, and they go a lot further back.

A lot of False Prophet can be traced to Normandi Ellis' translation of the Egyptian Book of the Dead, "Awakening Osiris".

The Egyptian Book of the Dead is pooled from ancient Egyptian Funerary texts dating back to around 2400 BCE.

Written in unique hieroglyphics, the texts at first were inscribed on the walls of the burial chambers of Pharaohs and Queens within the pyramids and were intended to aid the dead in taking their place among the Gods.

By 1070 BCE, the texts were more commonly written and distributed on papyrus and were no longer exclusively reserved for Kings.

Dylan had previously quoted often from ancient texts but surely none more ancient than this.

Some quotes are direct, "I opened my heart to the world and the world came in" and "my lungs fill with the breath of fire. A cool breeze encircles me" and some are more indirect.

The narrator in Awakening Osiris describes the birth of the Gods and all the world, in False Prophet the narrator "knows how it happened, I saw it begin"; in Awakening Osiris, the narrator is full of bravado and self-aggrandisement and begins many passages with "I am" and so does Dylan in the swaggering False Prophet.

In the ancient text and in the song, separated by thousands of years, both narrators are walking from one scene to the next, commenting on what they witness and who they're with while building themselves up. They are both seemingly written from outside of time, too. Dylan's narrator remembers neither when they were born nor when they died and the one in Awakening Osiris is reborn anew each day.

Underneath all this is another appropriation. False Prophet is propelled along by both the music and the melody of Billy "The Kid" Emerson's 1954 B-Side If Lovin' is Believing.

This is not the first time Dylan has meshed together direct literary influences with old-time music. "Love and Theft" is filled to bursting with quotes from Junichi Saga's compelling and captivating 1991 memoir Confessions of a

Yakuza while elsewhere on the album, some songs are so close musically to obscure older recordings – Sugar Baby to Gene Austin's The Lonesome Road and Tweedle Dee & Tweedle Dum with Uncle John's Bongos by Johnny and Jack – that they are essentially covers.

On Modern Times, Dylan was at it again. When the Deal Goes Down is an unlikely melting pot of Bing Crosby's Where the Blue of the Night (Meets the Gold of the Day) and several poems by Civil War poet Henry Timrod.

Set to the melody of Crosby's signature tune, Dylan tweaks lines such as "A round of precious hours

Oh! here, where in that summer noon I basked

And strove, with logic frailer than the flowers" into something entirely new and entirely his own.

Repeating the feat three songs later, Beyond the Horizon marries Bing Crosby's Red Sails in the Sunset and Henry Timrod's poetry again. This is perhaps Dylan's neatest tying together of such disparate sources as the line recounting the sweet sound made by the Bells of St Mary's can be seen as a reference to either Timrod's poem Katie or to Crosby's 1945 film The Bells of St Mary's.

∞

A week before Rough and Rowdy Ways is released an interview with Dylan appears in the New York Times.

The headline ran "Bob Dylan Has a Lot on His Mind" and indeed what followed was a ranging, meandering conversation about his new record, about living by the ocean and blue mind, Little Richard's Gospel music and the murder of George Floyd, which happened in Dylan's home-state and sparked a worldwide movement; "It sickened me no end to see George tortured to death like that," he said. "It was beyond ugly. Let's hope that justice comes swift for the Floyd family and for the nation."

It was not just the murder of George Floyd that caused outrage the world over. The sickening images that circulated that day, the actions of those police officers, was the latest in a long line of sickening, indefensible and perverse murders of black human beings at the hands of American law enforcement.

Before George Floyd there was Breonna Taylor, shot dead in her own home while she slept by police officers who had forcefully entered for no clear reason. Before Breonna Taylor there was Atatiana Jefferson who was shot and killed by police in front of her eight year old nephew while she was in her own home following a report from a neighbour that her front door had been left open. Before Atatiana Jefferson was Stephon Clark, Botham Jean, Philando Castile. There was Alton Sterling, Freddie Gray and Walter Scott. Janisha Fonville, Aura Rosser, Eric Garner, Michael Brown and Michelle Cusseaux and Gabriella Nevarez, Akai Gurley, Tanisha Anderson and twelve-year-old Tamir Rice.

Even still, it is not just the murders of countless black Americans that sparked such impassioned outrage but the institutional and systematic racism which is so deeply rooted into all facets of our society and into the police forces the world over. It is hard to see how it can be eradicated except by wholesale systemic change.

As protests broke out in downtown Minneapolis where George Floyd was suffocated to death by Derek Chauvin, the police response was disproportionate and served only to escalate tension between the state and its people.

Civilians who came out to protest had acted as peacefully as can be given the level of emotion and tension and were greeted with tear gas, rubber bullets, beatings and arrests. The police saw a protest against their own violence and decided that more violence was the answer. Another case in point that things can not continue as they are and that something has got to change.

As the reporting of the events switched the language from "protesting" to "rioting", the streets filled up with bodies, placards, bullets and smoke. Bob Dylan looked down over Minneapolis; the mural that had recently been painted of him declaring that "The Times They Are A-Changin'" acting as a backdrop to the largest Civil Rights Movement since the 1960s, when that particular song had first been written. Dylan was in fact part way through recording the The Times They Are a Changin' album when he performed at the March on Washington; the day Martin Luther King Jr gave his legendary I Have a Dream speech.

Some things change, some things stay the same. Unfortunately for everyone who has been killed, or is, horrifically, still to be killed by the police, the times are not changing fast enough.

∞

This is the backdrop to which Rough and Rowdy Ways entered the world on June 12, 2020; in the midst of a deadly pandemic and with protests and violence in the streets of cities the world over; indeed, that very day Rayshard Brooks was gunned down by police in Atlanta, Georgia.

The album acted, for me at least, as something of an escape and a release. It sounds as if it was recorded in another world, outside of time. A world that is softer at the edges than the corporeal one. There is still injustice, evil and death but in this world that Dylan creates and inhabits there is serenity and tranquillity, too. He is the ferryman that offers us safe passage across the river of blood and on into his world where time and space do not exist.

On the day it was released, I woke up and immediately left home to head for Rough Trade East. On the bus I passed through Elephant & Castle and countless shops which had been boarded up; ghosts of business lost to the pandemic, whose windows were now being used to hang posters for Rough and Rowdy Ways.

Walking up Brick Lane there were yet more posters, either side of a huge United Against Racism mural. I ducked inside Rough Trade East, the third customer to make it through the doors that day since they'd opened and made a beeline for Dylan's new release. I picked up Phoebe Bridgers' Punisher, also released that day and also a masterpiece, and hurried home past the posters to listen to my new treasures.

Two of the three lead singles lead the album, I Contain Multitudes acting as Dylan's manifesto and statement of intent for the next seventy minutes of music, and then comes My Own Version of You.

On it, Dylan is Frankenstein and he is conjuring the future from the past; weaving together Scarface Pacino and Godfather Brando, Roman history and Shakespeare to build the ultimate creation.

Its descending riff is insistent and propels the song on, the speed at which Dylan rattles off his lines is startling and yet makes them no less powerful. The music is ominous, the lyrics are eerie and Dylan's performance perfectly encapsulates that mood.

It moves into the gorgeous, lamenting and sincere I've Made Up My Mind to Give Myself to You; Dylan is wandering the wilderness from sunrise to dawn, sticking around 'til the crowd has thinned out and declaring the love that only he has permission to grant to his unnamed subject. He takes a guitar solo that is pure Chess Records and comes back in with a prayer that the Gods will go easy with him and wraps up one of his greatest latter day love songs.

Black Rider could be the creation he sang about in My Own Version of You; its parts are drawn from all time.

He weaves Awakening Osiris into his work again, "I look back. The straight road behind me changes. It twists and twines beneath a night without stars. Is it even the same road I travelled a moment ago?" is condensed in Dylan's own hand, and from the same book, the narrator of the text mentions having witnessed a body severed in two, just as Dylan threatens to do to the Black Rider.

Woven together with The Egyptian Book of the Dead is the unlikeliest of Juvenal quotes – "the fantastic size of your cock will get you precisely nowhere" – with a nod to the Richard Rodgers showtune Some Enchanted Evening (recorded by Dylan on 2015's Shadows in the Night) and the traditional murder ballad, Duncan and Brady (recorded by Dylan for a scrapped 1992 album with David Bromberg).

It is this intertextuality that makes Dylan's work so rich, gives it such depth and leads so many fans to delve into what he has written. It is what gives so much opportunity to explore further reading and listening; Dylan is signposting his interests and leading us into realms we may not have otherwise stumbled.

Goodbye Jimmy Reed up next is a rollicking blues stomper that wouldn't have been out of place on Blonde on Blonde. In a 60 Minutes interview with Ed Bradley in 2004, Dylan claimed that he could no longer write like he used to but that he could do other things now. Here, though, he is flexing his muscles and showing that when he wants to appear, that Thin, Wild Mercury Dylan is still living inside of him.

What a thrill it would be to hear this, or indeed any song from the record, live in concert. What a riot it would be to hear Dylan declare he can tell a Proddie from a mile away in person and drawl that he thought he could resist her, but that he was *way* wrong.

"Sing in me, o Muse", begins Homer's Odyssey, "and through me tell the story of that man skilled in all ways of contending; the wanderer, harried for years on end". Perhaps no one in western music history can claim that the muse has sung in them with more authority than Bob Dylan, and in Mother of Muses he is falling in love with Calliope.

The song may well have been sparked by looking at his Nobel medal for the first time back at the Stockholm Waterfront in 2017, with its engraving of a poet recording the song of a muse. Perhaps this song is what they were singing, Dylan has merely written it down.

As it progresses, Dylan ties the time between then and now; joining the end of a chain of events that started with civil war generals, on to Elvis Presley and Martin Luther King and concluding with a nod to Leonard Cohen's perfect swan song; "I'm travelling light, and I'm slow coming home".

Tying himself to history even further back, Dylan crosses the Rubicon next on the fourteenth day of the most dangerous month of the year; the Ides of March and the assassination date of Julius Caesar (of My Own Version of You fame).

The off-mic "oh, lord" between the penultimate and final verse puts me in mind of the more candid side of Dylan last seen on record on 2009's Together Through Life as he laughs and whoops his way through It's All Good.

Once the rumble and dust of Crossing the Rubicon has floated down the river, Key West (Philosopher Pirate) rolls in on the hazy wind and blows over you and blows you over.

It is one of those songs that has always existed; it's everything Dylan has always been singing about. Hearing it for the first time is like hearing it for the hundredth time and when you get to your hundredth listen it's like you're hearing it with new ears, reborn again. It is the penultimate triumph on an album of triumphs.

∽

Predictably, the album is compared to what has gone before; "his best since Tempest" or since "Love and Theft", depending on which latter day Dylan album the commentator prefers. "The best since Blood on the Tracks" for those who are given to looking further back.

The album, though, stands by itself; in Dylan's discography and in anyone else's. There are comments that the quality of his singing and that the sparse arrangements are a result of his foray into the Great American Songbook, but this album has its roots set deeper than any of the sixty or so standards Dylan recorded.

Dylan's singing is of course noteworthy, but then his singing always has and always will be noteworthy.

The music is exactly as it should be on the album. Matt Chamberlain has replaced long time band member George Receli at the drums and Bob Britt adding guitar where once Stu Kimball played – both having joined Dylan's live band on his fall tour of North America in 2019 and lending their talent to new arrangements of Lenny Bruce and Not Dark Yet – and Alan Pasqua, Fiona Apple, Blake Mills and Benmont Tench add their talent, too.

Chris Shaw, who produced "Love and Theft" is back in the studio control booth and has done a fantastic job in making the record sound as good as it does; False Prophet is the closest I've ever heard Dylan sound on an album to being in the room listening to him perform.

Recorded over a couple weeks at Sound City Studios in January and February of 2020, it's lucky that Dylan, his band and everyone involved in the record managed to make the sessions happen when they did, before the world began to shut down a month later.

It is hard to compare Dylan albums to one another simply because he is a new artist with each release but this may be the most complete, the most singular Dylan yet; the mastery of his art complete for now until he unveils the next Bob Dylan.

He may not be shifting the culture of music in his 70s anymore, he may not be blazing the trails but I think as an artist Dylan is more important than ever.

His work is more grounded, it's more real and emotionally resonant, even if he remains as far away as ever. The work he has released since 1997's Time Out of Mind is in a class of its own and will endure just as much, if not more, than classics like Bringing It All Back Home, The Freewheelin' Bob Dylan and Blonde on Blonde. You need only listen to the staggering Rough & Rowdy Ways to see that he has lost none of his powers.

To my ears, "Love and Theft" is the single greatest American record of all time. Rough and Rowdy Ways may be even more perfect.

Each stand outside of what else was going on at the times of their release – the former released on September 11, 2001 and the latter announced weeks into a pandemic – and both will endure for as long as people are listening to music.

But that's not to dismiss his earlier records. It's easy to forget about all those that came in between his 60s output and his 21st Century revival, too. Street-Legal, Saved, and Shot of Love are among some of my favourite of Dylan's albums. Each are underappreciated outside his fanbase and each deserve to be talked about more.

That they get lost in discussion about Dylan's best work among albums like Highway 61, Blonde on Blonde, Blood on the Tracks, Desire, Time Out of Mind, "Love and Theft", Tempest and Rough and Rowdy Ways says more about the mind-boggling consistency and talent of Bob Dylan than it does those particular albums.

∞

With the new album out, it's hard to listen to anything else.

Bob Dylan has given his fans something to cherish and to cling to while the world goes by outside our window and grows black before our eyes.

I supplement continual listening with endless YouTube videos; of the funk infused Can't Wait from Hyde Park last year, where Dylan dances through the song to the surprise of everyone in the comments section and to the ethereal, defiant rendition of Not Dark Yet from the fall tour. I've lost count of the amount of times I've watched Dylan's duet with Neil Young from Kilkenny last year where they sang Will the Circle Be Unbroken? together. Dylan's vocal is sublime.

I watch Dylan's defiantly cool, swaggering performances of Blind Willie McTell from the Annual Critics' Choice Movie Awards ceremony in 2012 and Cold Irons Bound from 2010; another 2012 clip of Dylan, this time goofing around on stage in Argentina during The Levee Gonna Break where he laughs and dances in ever more exaggerated ways as the song goes on and what is, to my ears, *the* definitive version of It's Alright Ma (I'm Only Bleeding), from Birmingham, England in 2007.

On September 16 he announces the return of his Theme Time Radio Hour show with a special episode to commemorate and advertise his Whiskey line.

Theme Time originally ran from 2006 to 2009 and was recorded on the road but presented as being taped in the (fictional) Abernathy Building.

Each show ran for an hour and was based around a theme – Baseball or The Bible, Texas or Tears, Cats or Cadillacs – where Dylan introduced a selection of related songs with a warmth, wit and enthusiasm that took a lot of listeners off guard. The series ran for one hundred episodes and must have spun a thousand songs by as many different artists.

The latest episode, recorded during lockdown, is perhaps the pick of the bunch and catches Dylan in the highest of spirits as he introduces songs from across a multitude of genres and eras, backgrounds and even languages each based around his favourite spirit. He cracks jokes, he shares truly fascinating insights into the songs he's playing and takes calls from friends. From the first second to the last the episode is an absolute treat.

I wonder what else he has been doing during lockdown. Whether he has spent his time painting, welding, reading, writing and recording new music. Perhaps he's been finishing up the follow up to his critically acclaimed 2004 memoir, Chronicles: Volume 1 – his original contract with Simon & Schuster was for six books – or maybe he has been spending time with loved ones.

It seems that he has been recording new music, at least, in the form of the soundtrack for Robert Clapsadle's movie, Hotel Refinement (there is very little information available about Clapsadle, but his one previous movie, 1999's Paradise Cove, is credited as featuring Dylan in the role of Alfred the Chauffeur. I am yet to meet or hear of anyone who has seen Paradise Cove, nor is it available anywhere to view online). Sometimes he really can be as mysterious as people will have you believe.

∞

Even without seeing Dylan during the year, his presence loomed large over 2020, or at least, over my year.

Seeing the musical based around his songs, building up to its release and then indulging on Rough and Rowdy Ways, chasing it with his Whiskey radio show and taking a trip to the now re-opened Halcyon Gallery to see his latest collection of artwork, Dylan seemed to be everywhere for me and all at once.

In December news broke that he had sold the publishing rights to his entire back catalogue to Universal in a deal worth between $300 million and $400 million; the biggest such deal ever made for a single artist's catalogue. It is hard to think of any others who will command a higher fee in future.

As the world tentatively began to re-open in March 2021, he was still inescapable and as his eightieth birthday approached, Dylan fever reached fever pitch.

In London and in Brighton I bumped into his artwork again and again in several galleries (including the Halcyon Gallery in London, featuring new paintings and lyrics that Dylan created during the pandemic, inspired by all the movies he had been watching); online, a heavy stream of articles appeared that were both pro and anti-Dylan and shelf-fulls of books were released to commemorate and celebrate his impending birthday. Previously unheard recordings – from 1962 and 1983 – appeared online and it turned out that Dylan Inc was gearing up to release another instalment of The Bootleg Series, this time focusing on his work between 1981 and 1985. In May, Dylan was even papped; he was caught by a photographer heading into the coffee shop he owns in Santa Monica, looking well and looking stylish in a short sleeved bowling shirt, dark trousers, biker boots and Ray-Bans. His fanbase online was abuzz with fresh activity each day.

It is, frankly, inconceivable that he has managed to move forward, push boundaries, stay relevant and stay creative for so long. What he has achieved in his life is simply monumental; all the songs and all the albums, all of the nearly four-thousand concerts performed and every mile covered to perform them; the staggering amount of artwork produced and the staggering way he has improved over the years, the books and the films, the poetry, the radio show and the welding, the charity and humanitarian work, running a café and a boxing-gym in Santa Monica, the whiskey and all the guest appearances on television and award shows, from Dharma & Gregg to The Grammys; every accolade he has received and all the projects we don't know about or those that nearly happened but ultimately didn't – the HBO sitcom with Larry Charles or the fragrance range – while still managing to find the time to raise a bunch of kids who call him pa in between it all. It was not a false proclamation, as he approached his ninth decade, to declare himself the enemy of the unlived, meaningless life.

∞

Rumours have begun to spread online that Dylan is gearing up to hit the road at the end of the year. Whether it will be safe to do so by then or not is yet to be seen, the pandemic may yet have other plans. I've had my vaccination, though, so whenever the green light is given, I'm ready to see him anywhere, if the good Lord willing and the creek don't rise.

∞

I'm standing in a park in North London watching a river flow; a family of swans are ferrying their cygnets across the water. I've just taken a photo and out of habit flick through my phone, open Instagram and see a post from the delightful Definitely Dylan page; one of the most important pages to follow if you are interested in engaging in Bob Dylan discussion online. The post says that Bob Dylan has announced a new show called Shadow Kingdom.

For the first time ever, he will be presenting his fans with a streaming concert.

"Shadow Kingdom will showcase Bob Dylan in an intimate setting as he performs songs from his extensive body of work, created especially for this event", the press release reads. "Shadow Kingdom will mark the first concert performance since December 2019, and first performance since his universally acclaimed album, "Rough and Rowdy Ways".

I have no idea what this is going to be like; whether he'll perform solo or with his band, whether he'll talk between songs or only sing, whether it'll be live or pre-recorded or whether we'll get close up camera angles or if he'll be drenched in darkness; whether there will be any new songs or covers, whether he is going to duet with any of his contemporaries or with any contemporary artists.

Before I can begin to contemplate the answer to any of these questions I have bought a ticket to the event. It doesn't matter what it's going to be like. I'll see him in anything, so I'll stand in line.

CHAPTER TEN

COLUMBIA RECORDING ARTIST, BOB DYLAN

Hammersmith Apollo. London, England. November 20, 2011
Hammersmith Apollo. London, England. November 21, 2011

My mum is standing in the doorway in the kitchen when I walk in. She has a piece of paper in either hand. She has Happy Birthday on her tongue.

She has just printed out the tickets to see Bob Dylan that she's purchased for my birthday in a few weeks' time. It doesn't feel real. I give her a hug and can't thank her enough.

Between now and the concert I barely think of anything else. I religiously watch clips on YouTube of recent performances; an incredibly shot Gonna Change My Way of Thinkin' from Tel Aviv, the camera gets so close to Dylan who is commanding and holding every note with a power that feels so of the earth and yet so otherworldly at the same time. He looks like a giant.

I've been watching a clip of breakneck Things Have Changed from Florence and it is ferocious. Zoomed right in on Dylan's face as he winces, smiles, pouts and bites his lip between lines, this is the most apocalyptic sounding music I can recall ever hearing.

Another clip on constant rotation is from Milan, a loose and funky Can't Wait where Dylan is cloaked in darkness whilst pacing from one side of the stage to the next with the microphone in his hand. He is teasing the audience, pointing at individuals in the front row and smiling their way, building up the excitement in the room with a repeated "I don't know, I don't know, I don't know, I don't know, I don't know, I don't know…", a pause while he turns to laugh with his drummer before coming back in on time with the topper, "how much longer I can wait".

Throughout the audience is riotous, Dylan has worked them up into a frenzy.

He gets to the end of the song and walks off into the darkness at the far side of the stage before half turning back to the crowd, nodding his approval to them and giving a clap of thanks for their participation.

Every day on the long journey to school I listen to a new bootleg, lately focusing on the great fun of his 1986 and '87 tours with Tom Petty and The Heartbreakers. Every journey ends with a ten minute walk from the bus-stop to the school gate through a leaf covered alleyway and every day I queue up Blind Willie McTell for the walk.

I couldn't be more excited for the show. We spend the day before the concert, my 17th birthday, walking around Camden Market. It's the first time I've been here and I'm thrilled to see the bridge Dylan leads a band of fans along in the video for 1993's Mississippi Sheiks cover, Blood in My Eyes.

I pick up a couple of hats to try and emulate my hero; one with a colourful flower and feather in the side to get as close to the one he wore on the Rolling Thunder Revue and a top-hat to match that in the aforementioned music video.

On the day of the show we join the already substantial queue at around 1 pm. The sky is blue but there's a chilly wind blowing and warm buzz of excitement in the air.

Before I was a Dylan fan I was obsessed with David Bowie and as an eight year old would stand in front of our television for hours on end watching his final Ziggy Stardust concert on DVD; a concert which took place at this very venue in 1973.

My grandad joins my mum and I just in time for the queue to start moving. A thick American accent drifts back to us from further along the line, "I just hope he plays Tambourine Man!"

Mark Knopfler opens the show. We're the second row in from the rail and the woman in front of me is crying out for Romeo and Juliet between every song, even more vociferously so when Knopfler picks up his resonator.

"Not tonight", he says but does play a gorgeous song which I don't know, not being familiar with his solo work. Of the songs I'm hearing for the first time tonight, those that grab me the most are Song for Sonny Liston with its insistent riff and the as-yet-unreleased Privateering but overall every track is alluring.

His piano player is extraordinary and the mix of blues, bluegrass, folk and shanties is a welcome surprise, and not at all what I was expecting.

The finest moment in his set, though, and the song that

draws the biggest reaction from the crowd is Brothers in Arms. The stage has filled with smoke but when he starts to play, and oh yeah the boy *can* play, Knopfler's guitar cuts right through it. His voice is wistful and hushed as he steps up to sing of these mist covered mountains and after seven or eight incredible minutes, it's hard to focus on the remaining two songs for thinking about Brothers in Arms.

The stage is being cleared and reset ahead of the main event. People are milling about all around us and chattering away. This is it. The last five years of listening to every recording, watching every movie, clips of concerts and interviews, reading every book and article that I can get my hands on has been building up to this.

"Ladies and gentlemen, please welcome Columbia Recording artist, Bob Dylan."

∞

I can't see anything; the house lights are off but there is a rumble on the stage. The drummer is pounding his bass drum, there's a wildcat roar coming from a couple of guitars and a sustained organ note.

Suddenly a marching beat kicks in and the mess of noise locks into something coherent. The lights come up and I am staring directly at Bob Dylan who has begun singing Leopard Skin-Pillbox Hat. He's holding the notes like Caruso. He's imperious, he's utterly captivating and commanding. I'm awestruck.

I turn first to my mum, then to my grandad and then back to Dylan and I don't take my eyes off him for the rest of the song. From where we're standing at the very front of the room, I couldn't have a closer or a clearer view of the artist at work. You've got to get up as near the teacher as you can if you want to learn anything.

He doesn't look like Bob Dylan. He doesn't look like anyone else, either, though. He is decked out in black and white cowboy boots, trousers with a Civil War General stripe down the side, a long frock blazer with sequined embellishments. A jewelled Bolo Tie. A goatee, a glint in his eye and a huge white hat. He is shorter than I expected and yet he is entirely enormous.

I'd spent weeks watching those clips, spent years listening to every available recording he's ever made and yet I didn't know what to expect. I've been warned by people that Dylan can't sing anymore, that you can't recognise what he's singing and that the songs don't sound how they're supposed to.

But this *is* how they're supposed to sound. This is what he sounds like, and he's singing incredibly. I've never heard music like this before. It sounds like the end of the old world and a beginning of a new one.

At the end of the song he walks to the middle of the stage and picks up a beaten up sunburst guitar. It's kicked into overdrive as he starts growling his was through It's All Over Now, Baby Blue. I manage to momentarily drag my eyes away from Dylan and across the stage. He wasn't lying when he said he was in a cowboy band; every man on stage looks like a riverboat gambler from the American West; there are pencil taches abound, porkpie hats and scraggly, shoulder length hair everywhere you look.

I notice that Mark Knopfler has snuck back on stage unannounced and he is trading guitar lines with Dylan;

Knopfler's fresh and clean guitar duelling with Dylan's swampy, fuzzy sound and imperfect playing.

He's barking this song. On the first number he really was belting the track, even missing the title phrase a few times because he instead was choosing to hold the last note of the line before, his vibrato and control over his singing sustaining through the bars. I wonder if it's a choice to growl and prowl his way through It's All Over Now, Baby Blue. It must be, considering the contrast with the vocal before it.

Things Have Changed kicks in; immediate, throttling and downright scary. His voice is a nightmare, but I love it. The music is fast but Dylan is faster. It strikes me for the first time just how *loud* the sound is. I can feel the drums rattling in my chest, I can feel the bass under my feet and Dylan's threatening voice is pounding in my skull.

Marlon Brando once said that the two loudest things he'd ever heard in his life were a jumbo jet taking off and Bob Dylan playing live. I can't imagine a jumbo jet coming anywhere close to this volume.

Dylan blows his first harmonica solo of the night to a roar of appreciation from the crowd. It's a hostile, dragon breath solo and he sings one more verse before kicking things up a gear with the harmonica again to see the song out.

I feel like I am floating. The room doesn't feel real. This is all too good to be true.

Somehow, though, it gets even better. Dylan runs a glissando up the keys, his Korg set to a soulful organ sound, and holds the final note. The guitarists trade a few stabs and flourishes, leading into the song and I have no idea what Dylan is about to start singing.

The next song, it turns out, is Tryin' to Get to Heaven and the performance is staggering. It is a saddening, beautiful song about heartbreak, loss and moving on from what has gone before. At my young age, I've never experienced any of these things, but the way that Dylan is singing it means I don't have to. In his voice I can hear exactly how they feel. When he sings, I know everything.

He's back to the sustained, impassioned singing from the first song, but now he's more emotive and he's singing more sweetly. These words are richer than on Leopard Skin-Pillbox Hat, clearly written by a man who has seen and been through more.

Mark Knopfler takes a solo before Dylan comes back in to let us know that he has been all around the world. He sounds like he is imparting everything to us that he's found or seen on his travels, and there's a lot to tell.

In the final verse Dylan warns that you may think you've lost everything but you will find out you can always lose a little more. Now older and wiser, it is a direct contrast and contradiction to the line from Like a Rolling Stone, "when you ain't got nothing, you've got nothing to lose". It's like the Dylans from fifty years apart are talking to each other.

There's a fill from the drums, the guitarist bends a note to close the song and my heart breaks; one note and yet he manages to wring so much feeling out of it.

When the lights come back on, Dylan is back at centre stage with his guitar around his neck. Knopfler is gone now and the band are rolling into Honest With Me.

Dylan grabs the microphone from its stand and pushes the guitar onto his hip like a gunslinger. There are a few jokes in the lyrics to this song but right now it feels more like a threat. Dylan is manoeuvring across the stage; shuffling one way before coming to a stop to make his point; crooked at the knee and doubled over, pushing his guitars neck towards the ground with one hand while dragging the microphone to his mouth with the other. He looks like a spider moving around its web, sensing the vibrations of its prey and he is going in for the kill. I'd be honest with him, too, because in this mood, there's no telling what he might do.

I want to turn and ask my family what they think but I am so focused, so transfixed and so in awe that I don't want to miss even a second. Neither of them are huge Dylan fans. My Grandad recently told me that his favourite song of Dylan's, though, is Tangled Up in Blue so once he's finished singing that I draw myself away from the stage to smile at him for having heard the song he most likely wanted to hear tonight.

Summer Days is a riot, the guitar lines burrowing inside your brain while Dylan tinkers away, seemingly playing his own song, on his keyboard.

When he yells that he's going to break the roof and set fire to the place as a parting gift, it doesn't feel that unlikely. At this volume, I'm surprised the roof is still holding on, anyway.

Blind Willie McTell is swaggering and it is haunting. Dylan sings that he can tell us one thing and that is that no one can sing the blues like Blind Willie McTell.

It may be true, but I can't think of anyone still alive who is singing them like Bob Dylan, either. He sounds more like Howlin' Wolf tonight, or maybe Willie Dixon, than he does Bob Dylan.

The volume, somehow, cranks up even further for an urgent Highway 61. I feel like the ground below me is going to split in two, the rumbling force from the stage too much for the room to bear. The song is swinging and Dylan is bouncing behind his keyboard, leaning in to sing his lines and then pulling away from the microphone to get lost in the incredible music his band is creating in front of us all.

Next up he tells us all about Desolation Row and everyone on it and warns us of the Thunder on the Mountain before directly addressing the crowd for the first time in the night.

"Well, thank you friends. I want to introduce my band right now", he drawls in an almost Southern accent and I wonder where that twang has come from in his voice considering he is from America's Midwest and lives out on the West Coast. "Over on the rhythm guitar, Stu Kimball. Donnie Herron, well he's playing on the steel guitar. Charlie Sexton, playing the electric guitar. George Receli, yeah he's playing on the drums and Tony Garnier is playing on the bass guitar."

I have a feeling that I'm going to be spending a lot of time with these six incomparable musicians from now on.

∽

The next night I'm back in the room with them again. I pooled all the money I got given for my birthday to buy a last minute ticket for the show.

Last night is all I've been able to think about all day. How could I think about anything else but that version of Things Have Changed? That version of Trying to Get to Heaven? Or the house of mirrors version of Ballad of a Thin Man, with its haunting echo effect at the end of every line, sounding like there were ten terrifying Dylans singing this song to us?

Tonight is the final night of Dylan's touring for the year. I have to be there.

When he walks onto the stage it feels just as magical as it did last night. It feels like I'm witnessing this man before me for the first time all over again and when he starts singing Leopard Skin Pill-Box Hat it doesn't matter that twenty-four hours ago I was in the same room hearing the same man singing the same song; tonight it is an entirely new and fresh experience.

It doesn't matter that the next two songs are the same, too, because they are alive and they are breathing and they might have the same names but they're new songs that the band are conjuring up on the spot.

Instead of playing Trying to Get to Heaven next they play Spirit on the Water and there is a buzz in the air the whole song through which finally bubbles over and erupts into a joyous "No!" from the crowd at Dylan singing "You think I'm over the hill? Think I'm past my prime?". I have goosebumps.

After Honest With Me comes a slow, funereal paced Forgetful Heart. Tony Garnier has moved to an upright bass and is playing mournfully with a bow. Dylan's singing is remarkable and emotive, moving and a world away from how intimidating it had sounded just one song before.

When he warns us that if it keeps on raining, the levee's gonna break I'm reminded of our proximity to the Thames. The volume that this band play at would be enough to crumble the walls around the river but I know that even if that happened and waves crashed through into the room, this band would keep on playing until they could play no more.

And play they do, with long extended and improvised blues movements between verses. You can't help but move and even Dylan is dancing on stage.

After the flood, Dylan heads back to centre stage and is back into intimidation mode. On the record, Man in the Long Black Coat is a song about being left by a woman; whether she has ridden off with a mysterious stranger or whether she has died is unclear, but tonight as Dylan sings it I realise that *he* is the man here tonight in a Long Black Coat. The snarl on his lips momentarily flickers into a smile before settling back and I feel that the point is not lost on him.

∽

All Along the Watchtower becomes Like a Rolling Stone and at this point last night the show was over. Tonight, though, Dylan keeps his hands pressed down on the keys and leans into the microphone to welcome Mark Knopfler back to the stage.

The crowd around me screams in appreciation when the first lines of Forever Young escape Dylan's lips. The atmosphere ramps up. There is a buzz in the air. I feel like I'm floating above the world. We all know we're seeing something special.

Knopfler takes the vocals on the second verse and then plays a gorgeous solo on his trademark red Stratocaster once he's finished singing.

Dylan takes control again for the third and final verse, sweetly singing the first two couplets and then he leans back to wait for the band to catch up with him before he sings the final lines.

Knopfler beats him to it, though, and jumps in. Dylan raises his head, looks across the stage. Behind them Tony Garnier leans in, watching expectantly and carefully to see how this moment will pan out and where to lead the band. "May your heart be always joyful" Knopfler sings and then turns side on to look directly at Dylan, "may your song always be sung". He lifts his hand towards the song's writer and the crowd *erupts*. The music for the last two nights has been thunderously loud but somehow the crowd is now louder. Tony Garnier bursts into a smile that could light the whole room and the two frontmen take the chorus together, trading Forever Youngs between them before Dylan claims centre stage all for himself with a final harmonica flourish.

※

Ever since he first started writing them, Dylan's songs have always been sung. They've been sung by Alicia Keys, and by Nina Simone; by Johnny Cash, Joan Baez and the Beatles. They've been sung by Wilco, Willie Nelson, Jimmy LaFave, Norah Jones and by My Chemical Romance; Solomon Burke, The Byrds and the Turtles; Bettye LaVette and Elvis Presley; by The Rolling Stones, Esther Phillips, Stevie Nicks, Joni Mitchell and Marianne Faithful; by Miley Cyrus, Rag 'n' Bone Man, Ed Sheeran, Ronan Keating and Morrissey. He's been covered by Burl Ives and by Jimi Hendrix, by Frankie Valli and Bobby Womack, the White Stripes and Green Day; Bryan Ferry, Adele and Warren Zevon. His songs have been sung by Sheryl Crow and by Tom Jones, by Sam Cooke and Rage Against the Machine, by Alanis Morissette and by Bette Midler, Bruce Springsteen and Tracy Chapman. By most everyone who has ever taken a guitar to a campfire, an open mic night or performed a solo concert in their bedrooms.

His songs have always *been* sung, and they *always* will be.

EPILOGUE

SHADOW KINGDOM

118th Street Coffee House. Santa Monica, CA. USA.
"July 18", 2021
(Or; The Bon Bon Club in Marseille. The Shadow Kingdom)

No-one knows what to expect. Even the co-founder of Veeps, the platform that will be airing the broadcast, Joel Madden seemed to be in the dark about what Shadow Kingdom would turn out to be. "We're here on the edge of our seats with everybody else," Madden says. "All I know about it is what everyone else knows: that he's putting together a show. There's renditions of songs that go back into his catalogue and from his new album. As a fan, I'm super excited to see what that means."

From the second Shadow Kingdom was announced, the online Dylan community went into overdrive. What would he play? Would he be solo or with his band? Would the stream be in black and white or colour? Would it be live or taped beforehand? Would there be an audience in the room? Is there any chance at all that we could hear brand new compositions, written during lockdown and will the show really only be available for 48 hours before it is cast into the wind?

There were rumours that he would be collaborating with "new, younger performers" which sparked more wild-fire speculation. Perhaps thinking back to Dylan's duets with Norah Jones at an off-circuit, pro-shot gig in 2005, guesses that he'd collaborate with Jack White, Fiona Apple or his Wallflower son Jakob show that Bob Dylan fans may just have their own definitions of words like "new" and "young".

Still, it would be a thrill to see Dylan recreate his collaboration with Fiona Apple on Murder Most Foul in a live setting or to perform publicly for the first time with his son.

My own personal wish-list for new, younger performers for Dylan to collaborate with would be more along the lines of Faye Webster or Phoebe Bridgers, Courtney Barnett or Angel Olsen, Alynda Lee Segarra or Zella Day. Perhaps a duet with Nathaniel Rateliff is not out of the question, considering the joint tour they were supposed to embark upon last year.

∞

I spent July 18th reading Michael Gray's Song & Dance Man: The Art of Bob Dylan from cover to cover, and it turned out to be appropriate pre-show reading.

Released in 1972, the book focuses on the early work of Bob Dylan and so does Shadow Kingdom.

There has been a huge buzz online all day. All anyone now knows is that the show is pre-recorded and that none of Dylan's touring band are involved.

Every Dylan fan with an internet connection is sat in front of the screen as the clock ticks into 10 pm GMT and the show is set to start. Another countdown appears and it seems we have ten more minutes until showtime. It is the first trick of the night from the ultimate trickster.

Eventually, the screen fades to black and then into a black and white shot of Dylan and his new band playing to a small audience in a small roadhouse bar. There are no drums in sight; only an accordionist, double bassist and two guitarists surrounding Dylan who is himself wielding an acoustic guitar – something not seen in performance since he made an appearance at The White House in 2010 to tenderly sing The Times They Are A-Changin'.

You can hear a harmonica blowing, too, but no one on stage is playing it. It doesn't matter. Nor does it matter that none of the guitarists are playing the notes we can hear. It is clear from the opening thirty seconds before the text "Shadow Kingdom" and then "The early songs of Bob Dylan" fill up the screen that this is going to be a piece of performance art, a movie; not just a concert played straight through as anticipated. It is all a masquerade.

Bob Dylan has his Bob Dylan mask on and his band are each wearing face coverings; a familiar sight in this pandemic world we live in (and a welcome one considering some of Dylan's contemporaries anti-vaccination, anti-lockdown and anti-mask stances). It makes them hard to distinguish – they are masked and anonymous – but it also makes them look like bandits from an old Western Movie, performing behind the greatest gambler, gunslinger and outlaw popular music has ever seen.

When Dylan starts singing, it is astounding how good his voice is sounding. Eighteen months off the road has clearly been good for his vocal chords, and he smoothly moves his way through a stop-start, rootsy version of When I Paint My Masterpiece.

On the opening song his voice at times sounds like it did way back in the early 60s; like it did on Talkin' Bear Mountain Picnic Massacre Blues or on I Shall Be Free #10. He looks about twenty years younger than he is. It's hard not to get emotional watching Bob Dylan releasing new work, pressing on into his 80s and trying something new; coming up with new arrangements of old songs and sounding as good as he does. Perhaps, sounding even better than he ever has.

It could be worth noting that Dylan's 1978 fever-dream movie Renaldo & Clara also starts with a live rendition of When I Paint My Masterpiece. Dylan may well be letting us know that what is about to come is as (un)real and disorienting as the scenes from that movie were, or he is setting out his intention to paint a masterpiece once again for us as the night progresses.

It's exciting not knowing what song is going to come next or what they will sound like. When I Paint My Masterpiece fades into a rollicking Most Likely You Go Your Way (And I'll Go Mine).

Dylan seems to be singing over the heads of the single row audience. His timing, his phrasing, his delivery is for the most part perfect; even when he stumbles on the words a couple of times he has the confidence to press on through as if that was exactly how things were supposed to have sounded.

He is practically bouncing as he sings, he is gesticulating widely – every "you" in the lyric is accompanied by a point into the crowd and every "me" and "I" has the singer pointing at himself.

Look closely at the end of the song, and you'll see that the audience has been replaced with mannequins looking up at Dylan. In 2019, the mannequins were part of Dylan's stage set-up; tuxedo and cocktail dress clad figures lining the back of the stage at every performance he gave on the Autumn / Winter leg of his tour.

Next up, Queen Jane Approximately sees a location and outfit change. No longer in the bar, it seems, they are now surrounded by curtains draped along the walls and equipment. Perhaps, this is the band staying on to play for themselves after closing time; or after the roadhouse has closed its doors for the final time.

It strikes me that these could each so far be stand-alone music videos. The performances have each stood alone, too. Each one sounds rich. The band are tight in all the right ways and loose in all the best. Dylan's voice is sublime. He has occasionally spoken about wanting to go back and record his old songs "properly" and with Shadow Kingdom, it feels like that is what he is doing. He is expertly and perfectly blending his old words with his new sound. He's only played Queen Jane Approximately seventy-six times in concert before this. Never once has it sounded better.

Just as enjoyable as hearing the music, is watching the pictures. As Queen Jane not so much finishes as falls apart, there is a cut to someone tapping their foot against the black and white tiles and another someone checking their cigarette and flicking their ash into a tray.

When the camera pulls back to the stage, the lights in the room are flickering across the guitarists' faces and their shadows are dancing on the wall. In this iteration, I'll Be Your Baby Tonight is a 50's dancehall bop. It cuts to Dylan, now dressed in white, who is playing guitar again and he is flanked on either side by two women who are looking directly down the barrel of the camera lens. One of the women brushes Dylan's shoulder. No one takes their eyes off the camera and none of us at home take our eyes off the screen.

At the end of the song the camera gets in closer to Dylan's face than any camera-operator has been permitted to in years. It lingers on the woman to his right before focusing entirely on Dylan who hollers one last title refrain while the lens flares with light and Dylan looks us dead in the eyes, a knowing smile dancing inside his own.

The camera moves to a shot of bodies dancing around the room, interestingly, between songs. Now there is tinsel around the top of the stage and the air is thick with smoke.

It seems that from here on in, the setup is going to become more and more staged; itself part of the performance, part of the illusion and part of the show.

Just Like Tom Thumb's Blues starts with a long shot of a photo of a sinking ship hanging on the wall. When it cuts to Dylan he is now sat among the crowd, facing the camera with his back to his audience.

This scene gives more than a nod to Dylan's 1964 performance on Quest, on Canadian TV Channel CBC; on both occasions he is surrounded by workmen and barroom regulars, none of whom seem to be paying him any mind.

If you can draw your attention away from Dylan for long enough, you can see that while everyone behind him is smoking and drinking, one actor is doing so in slow motion. It takes him the whole first verse just to take his cigarette from behind his ear and put it to his lips.

Dylan's Santa Monica café, the 118th Street Coffee House, where the movie was filmed (later credited as The Bon Bon Club in Marseille, which is right around the corner from Theme Time Radio's Abernathy Building), looks like it could be an old run down bar in an Oklahoma dustbowl.

It looks like he's in a saloon in the old American West. He looks like he's performing in the middle of Tike and Ella May Hamlin's run down shack in Woody Guthrie's only complete novel, House of Earth. He could just as easily be performing in Kate Trask's whorehouse from John Steinbeck's monumental East of Eden.

Equally, he could be playing in the boarding house from Conor McPherson's Girl From the North Country. Wherever he is, wherever he's supposed to be, there's no doubt that he's back in that old, weird America. He is everywhere, and all at once.

At times, Dylan could be Humphry Bogart navigating a scene in a classic film noir picture in Hollywood; he could be the Merchant of Menace, Vincent Price, stalking the Shadow Kingdom.

He looks most Price-esque on Queen Jane and again on the next song, Tombstone Blues. Back in the curtained room setting, it is a completely reworked song. The pace is slowed right down and Dylan stands off to the side of the staging area to deliver the words with power. It's more of a reading of a piece of poetry than it is him singing a song.

The next song is another total re-working, this time lyrically as well as musically. To Be Alone With You is transformed from a crooned come-on, to more of a threat (lyrically, but also as Dylan spends much of the song with his fists raised like a boxer, either side of the guitar that hangs from his neck).

Dylan sounds pleading and ghostly on new lines such as, "I'll hound you to death, that's just what I'll do / I won't sleep a wink, til I'm alone with you" and, continuing his 21st Century obsession with violence, murder and lawlessness, "What happened to me darling? What was it you saw? / Did I kill somebody? Did I escape the law?". Outside of perhaps Nick Cave or Tom Waits, there aren't many others who could transform a lounge-love song into a murder ballad.

Dylan flips the subject of mortality from his true love's to his own, as he emphatically repeats "*my* mortal bliss, is to be alone with you" to finish the song.

The way this performance has been shot and with the new lyrics about murder and the outgunning-and-outrunning the law, this version of To Be Alone With You could almost act as a sequel to the film noir video for 2015's The Night We Called It a Day; where Dylan can be seen escaping the scene of a double murder – that of his love rival in the piece and his lover.

Behind him on the wall a clock stays stuck at 10:12 (presumably, pm). Either the seconds don't pass in the Shadow Kingdom or else they would, if Bob Dylan didn't keep stopping time with incredible performance after incredible performance.

Dylan is using every voice he's ever sung with tonight; his smooth croon, his Rolling Thunder holler, his older-than-his-years balladeering from his first record, his nasal, taunting drawl from the mid-60s, his wolfman growl of the 00s, his bluegrass moan last heard on 1997's The Lonesome River duet with Ralph Stanley and the next song, What Was it You Wanted, gets his talk-singing treatment.

Not performed by Dylan since 1995, What Was it You Wanted sounds like one of those songs that has always existed or which is always being performed, just out of earshot in a shadow-realm. His care with the lyric is impeccable, his phrasing is exactly how it should be.

It is funny that Dylan's career is now so long that a song from 1989 could be considered for inclusion in a show subtitled "The early songs of Bob Dylan". Perhaps the title phrase is his way of teasing his audience who have spent the last month speculating wildly online about what Shadow Kingdom would be and what it is that we wanted.

Next up is perhaps the standout performance of the entire show; one of Dylan's most tender songs sang in one of his most delicate, considered and moving vocal performances of his entire sixty year career.

Forever Young was written for his son Jesse in 1973. Since then, it has become a universal ode to love, humanity and the human spirit. Indeed, Dylan has spent a lot of the last six years singing American Standards. Tonight, he is proving beyond any doubt that the songs in his own catalogue have all the hallmarks and quality, all the endurance to become Standards themselves, and none have this quality more than Forever Young.

All through the show, the musicians have switched up the instruments they're miming on. During Forever Young, Dylan is wonderfully backed by his own and one other guitar, double bass and a cascading dolceola melody. His voice is beyond description. I would be surprised if there were many dry eyes left among the tens of thousands tuning in around the world at the song's end. This is now the standard by which every other version of the song will be measured.

During the next song, Pledging My Time, the actors making up the audience are dancing across the front of the screen; Dylan is blocked from view occasionally as they slow-dance to the slowed down version. It is a perfect metaphor for Dylan's career and the impact of his music. He is there, pledging his time to us, soundtracking every event; standing in the shadows and sometimes just out of view, yet always looming large over our lives.

I wonder what songs we are yet to hear; how many more will be fit in to the movie's setlist. The Wicked Messenger, from 1967's John Wesley Harding album, is not one I was expecting but that is up next and it is the first version of the song I have heard and enjoyed.

Dylan is mostly visible throughout only as a silhouette; often the lighting in the room is flickering elsewhere as he sings the tale of a wicked messenger come from Eli. Between verses, a guitarist steps right in front of the camera, cigarette in his Fender's headstock, plays a riff and steps out of view again. It is a comedic action that lifts the tension from the song's lyric and a wonderful piece of cinematography.

Just when you think you understand what is going on, the rug is pulled from under your feet. At times, various band members stare directly at the camera. I wonder what the setting is supposed to be, what it means when they stare so deliberately and so unblinkingly at the lens.

Watching the River Flow begins to roll out of the speakers and the venue is now in full party mode; there are actors dancing on the floor or leaning around the stage sipping beers and smoking heavily. The lights are flickering every-which-way and the tinsel tassels around the stage are blowing. Dylan's voice is remarkable as he holds the notes. At times, all we can see of him is the light shining from behind him through his curly hair. He's a ghost in the shadows. He will be singing these songs for us for the rest of time.

Towards the end of the song he casts his gaze upon his dancing audience, leaning his microphone stand away from him to reveal his face. Coming out of the speakers is a guitar solo so obviously played by Dylan that the guitarist miming on-stage behind him even has room to take his hands away from his Fender to readjust his mask.

As Dylan watches on, the camera begins to move through the dancing bodies before him. Everyone is smiling, everyone is moving and grooving. We are transported into the cover art of last year's Rough and Rowdy Ways; where a well-dressed couple are dancing in an underground night club on Cable Street in London, in 1964.

When the song ends, the crowd stop dancing and start applauding those on stage. We can't hear the sounds of their clapping, it is a silent motion; just like Dylan, the band, the actors and the cast can't hear us at home appreciating the movie they have created for us.

What fun this must have been to be involved with.
What fun it must have been to put together.
What an absolute joy it has been to watch.

∽

The movie, and it is more of a movie than a concert, is perhaps Dylan's defining cinematic achievement. It is a formula he has been tinkering with since the music video for Sweetheart Like You in 1984; playing to no-one in-particular in an undisclosed location in Anytown, USA. At times, the shots are reminiscent of his performance of Cry a While at the Grammys in 2002, where his band are crammed into a box of shadows; at other times it recalls the musical sections of Masked and Anonymous, his 2015 Letterman appearance or his 2016 performance of Once Upon a Time at a tribute event to Tony Bennett.

In a 2009 interview with Rolling Stone, Dylan said, "At a certain point we'll take songs into the studio and we'll do a television show – television, like that still exists – with this band performing some kind of a repertoire of these particular songs. And they'll be recorded properly." That certain point, it seems, was now.

Director Alma Har'el has done a fantastic job of capturing Dylan the mysterio, the oddity, the ghost performer. She has done an incredible job of bringing thirty years of his experimentation to wonderful fruition, alongside Director of Photography Laurie "Lol" Crawley, Designer Ariel Vida, Art Director Kati Simon and her team Kira Kelly and Joshua Zucker-Pluda. Natasha Newman-Thomas pulled a perfect costume design together and the sound was sumptuously captured and mixed by Mike Piersante, Alex Somers and Paul Wingate. The choreography comes from Dominique McDougal. Owing to not only Dylan's incredible performance, but each and every cast member, Shadow Kingdom is a remarkable and singular achievement.

There turned out to be no collaborations with "young, new artists" in the sense that we'd been speculating, but the all-new band played behind and played off Dylan incredibly. The on-screen band was made up of Janie Cowan, Joshua Crumbly, Buck Meek, Shahzad Ismaily and Alex Burke. We may not know whether or not they were actually playing, and the plot thickened when guitarist Tim Pierce revealed in an interview that *he* had been involved with the recording of thirty songs for the film.

It's hard to imagine that when Dylan makes it back out onto the road that he won't have his regular touring band in tow, but, this group of musicians, whoever they were, will always be playing behind him in the Shadow Kingdom.

∽

Before the end credits roll, though, there is time for one more gorgeous performance to close out the film. Yes, and it's all over now, Baby Blue.

"That's my story, but not where it ends"
Bob Dylan, 2020

ENCORE

THE LAST OF THE BEST

The Beacon Theatre. New York, NY. USA. November 19, 2021
The Beacon Theatre. New York, NY. USA. November 21, 2021

It's just before 8pm on November 2nd, 2021, and a little under 2,500 people are taking their seats in the Riverside Theatre, Milwaukee, WI. Around the world, fans are logging into twitter and expectingrain.com, getting ready for the show, hoping for updates to trickle through. For the first time since 2019, we're going to the carnival tonight after over eighteen months of exile on Desolation Row.

Bob Dylan takes to the stage and performs for a live audience for the first time since December 6, 2019. I can only imagine the excitement and energy in the room. Not since the late 60s became the early 70s has Dylan's return to the stage been so anticipated, so defiant and so in doubt.

In the room the audience are being treated to reworked versions of Dylan deep cuts and the live debuts of almost every track from last year's monumental Rough and Rowdy Ways.

Online, those of us who are tuning in from all around England, Germany, Australia, America and Canada, Japan, Austria, Italy and beyond are working ourselves into a frenzy at the songs being played. The always fantastic photographer Duncan Hume, lucky enough to be in attendance, is tweeting out the setlist – "River Flow", followed a few minutes later by "You Go", then simply "Multitudes", "False P", "Twist" and on through the night until reaching the final performance, "Takes a Lot".

Those of us who are watching the show without having any way of watching the show are all as excited as if we had front row seats; we discuss what song will be next, which lines will get the best reaction, who the new band members are, what the new arrangements could sound like and which songs will get new lyrics. We talk about the amount of new material being performed, which songs from Shadow Kingdom are being played and agree that the true wildcard of the night is Melancholy Mood, resurrected from the Sinatra years.

The community spirit and communal excitement is intoxicating and giddying. We're all experiencing this together, but what is this? We can't see or hear anything. There aren't even any photos floating about online yet, and not a hint of a clip or video.

Several times over the last two years, the online Dylan community has come together like this; from the release of Murder Most Foul and build up to Rough and Rowdy Ways, to group watching and mass commentary of Dylan's maligned 1986 film Hearts of Fire; the release of the Whiskey episode of Theme Time Radio Hour, Shadow Kingdom and the latest excellent archival release, The Bootleg Series Volume 16: Springtime in New York. Dylan has brought us all closer through the hardest period and that has culminated tonight with his return to live performance.

Towards the end of the show at the Riverside, someone in the audience strikes up a live stream from their phone and the numbers of people watching online quickly dwarfs the amount of people physically in attendance.

The feed picks up just in time to capture Dylan talking to his audience, introducing his band and dedicating the night's performance to Les Paul, who was from around Milwaukee way.

The pandemic may be far from over but knowing that Bob Dylan has been back on stage; has performed to a live audience and is keeping on keeping on makes the world feel a little bit more normal than it did even just twenty four hours ago. It is like a natural order has been restored.

∽

Ever since the run of twenty one tour dates were announced, I'd been refreshing the news constantly; waiting to hear if the travel restrictions into America would be lifted by the time Dylan made his way to New York.

Eventually the date was confirmed, from November 8th, vaccinated travellers would be able to enter the United States for the first time in eighteen months, and that is just what we have done; touching down in New Jersey after the borders re-opened; making our descent as the full moon was rising, switching places with her in the sky.

An hour in a yellow taxi from Liberty International Airport allows us plenty of time to watch Manhattan grow and grow as we edge closer. We have a perfect view of the islands skyline across the Hudson river, with the moon looming large over the buildings that in turn tower over everything below.

Across the George Washington Bridge and into Harlem, we pay the taxi fare and climb the four steep flights of stairs to our Airbnb.

The door creaks open ominously and what online looked like a cool, arty space that felt perfect for a few nights in New York to see Bob Dylan in person feels like nothing short of a murder house. It feels like entering the scene of a crime; one that has either already been committed or is just about to be.

A scream rings out from the stairwell, a siren blares by the broken window and the light in the room flickers on and off, intermittently revealing the flies in the air.

Scribbled on the walls in untidy, crazed writing – some done with spray paint, some in red tape, some it seems simply done in Biro – are phrases like "ONE NATION", "I LOVE YOU MORE GOD!" and "LOVE MY LIFE", covering the space from the fireplace through to the fridge. Some of the writing in tape seems to have been clawed and scratched away in places.

The lock in the door doesn't seem to stick, the floors are uneven and creaking and so within ten minutes of being in the room we are looking for alternative accommodation. Another ten minutes on and we are on our way to Times

Square; to a much more conveniently located and, more importantly, less terrifying place to stay.

∞

Today, the wait is finally over. Twenty-eight months since I last saw him, I am going to be back in the room with Bob Dylan. Considering everything that has happened in that time period, it doesn't feel real.

I open my birthday presents and we head out; back into Times Square and up past Radio City Music Hall to Rockefeller Plaza. We head to the Top of the Rock and are blown away by the huge expanse of Manhattan, sprawling out in all directions. From up here, the buildings look even bigger than when you're standing in their shadows on the streets. New York feels like a theme park; a city where everything is bigger, wider, taller, higher than you're expecting it to be and where reality and expectations can't be suspended enough.

It's a beautiful day and once we're back on the ground we continue walking and exploring, stumbling into Bloomingdales. Playing a game of "guess the price" where even the most exaggerated estimate is usually dwarfed by the reality. Even the price tags here are larger than life.

We carry on up into Central Park, beautiful in the autumn as the leaves have blanketed the ground in warm yellows, oranges and reds. We take our time passing the park benches with dedications etched into them; memories of loved ones lost, declarations of love and a proposal that must have been impossible to refuse.

We see the Alice in Wonderland statue, complete with Alice and her pet cat Dinah, the Cheshire Cat, Mad Hatter,

Dormouse and White Rabbit. Crafted in 1959 by José de Creeft, the statue looks remarkably like the illustrations drawn by and from Lewis Carroll's 1865 classic.

We just have time for a quick pit-stop to grab a vegan burger, quickly run around the Times Square Disney store and head to the hotel to change into our evening best before it's time to walk up Broadway, to the Beacon Theatre and to see Bob Dylan.

∞

The lights in the cavernous hall of New York's Beacon Theatre are on bright, illuminating the intricately carved gold ceiling; the beautiful architecture and artwork. It's a beautiful room, full of life, a weight of history and culture. On stage, a barroom piano is set up front and centre, facing the audience; a drum kit on a riser is off to the audiences left and guitars are lined up across the rest of the stage. A buzz is in the air as the murmur of fans milling about fills up the rest of the space in the room.

At a couple of minutes past eight the lights go out and the room howls. Shadows are drifting onto the stage. The band kicks in before the lights underneath their feet flicker on. There they are. There he is. A shiver runs down the spine of every person in the room as Bob Dylan is illuminated before us as if he appeared out of nowhere.

It takes the sound engineer a couple of minutes to find their levels and so we miss the first two lines of the opening song. "What's the matter with me, I don't have much to say", Dylan had sung, if we'd been able to hear it.

The music was immediately loud and clear, though, and the effect it has on you after so long away is heightened, that electrifying thrill. Four thousand miles away from my house, I immediately feel at home.

Watching the River Flow is rollicking hillbilly hoedown tonight. The insistent cascading riff from the Shadow Kingdom is really being teased out on one of the guitars and it's impossible not to move your body in time to the music, even if we are confined to our chairs in the balcony. When Dylan sings the new lyric about his true love loving older men (she can't resist their charms), there is a ripple of laughter from the audience – is he acknowledging his age or has she got her eye on someone beyond even his eighty years?

The song stomps to a finish and after a few seconds kicks into a strutting, teasing Most Likely You Go Your Way (And I'll Go Mine).

Some of Dylan's teasing, taunting inflections come out as he sharpens some words and drags others out. It's the voice he sang with in the 60s when this song was written; that sneering, arrogant and cocksure Dylan is alive and kicking. Some lines have a descending staccato vocal melody, the way he'd have sung it in 2005. Some lines have sustained notes, the way he'd sing it in 2019. A growled "yeah" proceeds some fire and brimstone, a flicker of the power of the version of this song that opens 1974's Before the Flood. In one song, Dylan has given us a tour of all of his vocal powers, using all of his voices.

My partner beside me is at her first Dylan show. She turns my way, beaming, "I can see why you have to keep coming back. I get it". It's the best thing she could have said.

The crowd is going wild at the end of the song but lulls into a hush as the opening guitar notes ring in I Contain

Multitudes, the first song tonight from Rough and Rowdy Ways. They cheer again as Dylan sings the first line, at the first refrain and at the mention of the British Bad Boys, the Rolling Stones.

At the fourth song, False Prophet, all hell breaks loose. Dylan, his band and the whole audience get truly rough and rowdy. Those swaggering guitar notes kick in and Dylan is centre stage, standing like a gunslinger in a showdown.

Reports from earlier in the tour suggested that Dylan has looked his age, frail and shaky on his feet but as he stands before us now he is towering, commanding and, to borrow his trick of referencing epic Greek poetry, he looks Godlike.

He is not so much as singing this song at first as it is bursting out of him. He is yelling, cajoling, hollering. His howling voice is like a hammer. He's bending at the knees, almost doubling over, as if to wring every last ounce of energy out of himself to deliver the lines.

He's leading us on, the crowd is going wild and it feels like the room could split with a combination of the ear splitting volume and frenetic energy. If it does, Mary-Lou, Miss Pearl and Bob Dylan will be our fleet-footed guides through the underworld that's being revealed to us.

Back at the piano, now and there's a musical break in the song that is crying out for one of the two guitars to take over and push this whole racket on to the next level, into the next circle but neither step forward to fill it. It's the first time tonight that a fleeting feeling of missing Charlie Sexton takes over.

During the next instrumental break, Dylan hammers his keys if neither of the guitarists want to fill in the blanks, but one follows in his wake and bounces off his playing before the vocals come back in and see out the song.

Donnie Herron moves to violin and the band swing into When I Paint My Masterpiece. Having been on the brink of the underworld or at the end of the world in False Prophet, now we're in an old world. It's the sound of a honkytonk at the end of the old Frontier West. Dylan's voice is back to being tender, sweet and crooning after the fire of False Prophet. Bob Britt is on acoustic guitar now and playing a walking 12-bar blues line between his rhythm parts. Herron's violin soars behind Dylan's piano and voice, which are the three dominant parts you can hear. Over the honkytonk swing, Dylan's piano is a combination of jazz and blues.

It strikes me that while his guitar solos have always had some level of economy to the notes he'd use – in his autobiography, Chronicles: Volume One, Dylan explains how in the 90s he developed a three-note guitar solo system – he is a lot happier to fill in every available space with notes when at the keys.

"Someday", he sings, "everything is going to be beautiful". Sitting here, in this room, with this company, it already is.

∞

Before these three miraculous Beacon shows, Dylan has played here twenty-eight times, all since 1990, including a seven night residency in 2018 where he gave shoutouts to all the famous faces in the audience; making Jack White stand and bow to the applause of the audience one night and requesting that Martin Scorsese make The First Temptation of Christ on another.

It was fitting for Dylan to make such a request in such a room; the Beacon was conceptualised by film producer Herbert Lupin in 1926, who brought in architect Walter W. Ahlschlager to design what was originally to be called The Roxy Midway.

During construction, though, Lupin's finances collapsed and his plans for the theatre and its sister venues fell through. Eventually, the building was finished and opened as The Beacon in 1929 thanks to financial intervention from Warner Theatres. Known as a movie palace at the time, evidently a theatre so big was too grand to just be known as a cinema.

The venue originally hosted both film and vaudeville performances and by the early 1970s was primarily used solely for movies, until it changed ownership and began hosting concerts and dramatic performances, too.

∞

We're in Greenwich Village. On this day, sixty years ago, a young Bob Dylan stepped into Columbia's 30th Street Studios to put down the first tracks on his first album. He most likely would have headed out from one of the houses we pass on Bleecker Street, or maybe on Jones or 4th or whichever house he happened to be crashing on the sofa in along these streets and headed uptown with his guitar across his back.

On this day, ten years ago, I was standing in line to see a much older Bob Dylan for the very first time at London's

Hammersmith Apollo. What a journey it's been in those ten years. What an experience it's been following him all the way from my hometown of London to his adopted hometown of New York.

This morning I went out to pick up coffee, got back to the hotel room and as I put the drinks on the desk my partner and I blurted out at the same time, "we have to go and see him again". So it was decided, we looked around online and picked up a couple of tickets for the show tomorrow, the final night in the three night Beacon residency.

Here in Greenwich Village, Dylan looms large but so does everything that went on before and around him, too. This isn't just where musicians came to pass the basket around the coffee houses to have their songs heard and make enough food to eat every night, but comedians and actors, too. In the Bitter End, Al Pacino has performed short plays before he made it big and these streets are where he met Robert De Niro for the very first time. George Carlin, Richard Pryor and before them Lenny Bruce played in rooms around here.

Alongside the notable names, Washington Square Park has always been a place of political activism, of thought and progressive ideals; people would bring a crate to stand on and their voices to reach out to those in the neighbourhood to join their movements towards a better world.

Greenwich Village has always been a hub of great minds, great spirits and great culture.

We turn off MacDougal, from Bob Dylan's old house of the early 70s and wander through the fabled streets of Greenwich Village to find Cornelia Street and stop outside

Taylor Swift's old house. The tradition of great artists being drawn to this area is still alive. Carrying on, we intersect with West 4th Street and an intersection between the history of my favourite songwriter and my partners.

We stop off for a few drinks in a run down Irish pub and I wonder whether The Clancy Brothers would have been in here to loosen up before performing in the Village, way back in the 50s and 60s. Sitting opposite from my partner, who is herself of Irish heritage, it feels like an appropriate place to have stumbled into for a pit stop.

Around us are the remnants of Halloween decorations; cobwebs and pumpkins, corn crops and skeletons but outside there's a feeling of Christmas in the air. We're caught between two holidays, just like Thanksgiving, which is only a few days away. I'm thankful to be here, considering the way the last year and a half has gone and thankful for the company I'm keeping this time around. Thankful she took the chance to get to New York while we can while there is still so much uncertainty about the chain of events playing out with the pandemic.

∞

We're inside the sprawling Metropolitan Museum of Art, a stunning building worthy of the treasures it keeps inside. It's like a time machine for all human life and creativity and you can lose hours, and probably even days, in here without too much trouble.

We start about as far back as the museum goes, marvelling at statues and artefacts from antiquity; terracotta vases, gemstones and jewellery from Ancient Greece and

Rome to statues of Herakles and Medusa, Amazons, Sirens and Muses.

There is not much recent work of interest to see in The American Wing, but a real delight can be found in a painting called Dance in a Subterranean Roundhouse at Clear Lake, California. Painted by French artist Jules Tavernier, the incredible work depicts a ceremony being held by the Elem Pomo peoples and masterfully uses light and colour to transport you into the roundhouse. With almost one hundred faces within, the painting makes you feel closer to the people it portrays than even the artifacts of theirs that have lasted – the clothes, shoes and totems – on display in the next room.

When we come to a few paintings by Edward Hopper I notice a similarity in style, or at least in mood and tone, with the more recent pieces produced by Dylan. There are also hints of influence in pieces by Paul Delvaux; Small Train Station at Night particularly would not be out of place in a Dylan exhibit.

Further on, we come to works by Monet and Van Gogh and again I'm thankful that my partner is here to point out to me the details and techniques used, the influence these works had on what came later and the stories of the artist. An artist herself, it is magical to listen and learn as she opens up her knowledge of a world I know very little about.

We head into an exhibition on Surrealism and most every piece captures our rapt attention. This is a room where nothing should make sense but everything does; where everything should throw your balance out and knock your footing but which really makes you feel sturdier where you stand than some of the more real to life, perhaps too real to life, pieces on display can.

The surreal works of Dali and Alice Rahon, Leonora Carrington and Samir Rafi open up in my mind's eye that same weird, inaccessible world that is revealed at a Dylan show; you recognise all the parts but they're being put together in a way you don't expect, something is happening there but you don't know what it is.

Once we are able to drag ourselves away from The Met, we head across Central Park to another time machine only this time we aren't travelling back one hundred years or one thousand, but sixty five million.

Everything in America is bigger than it is back home, and the same is true for the dinosaurs on display at the Museum of Natural History. Immediately inside, an Allosaurus is frozen in battle with a Diplodocus – my two favourite dinosaurs together, reminiscent of a great hunt scene from BBCs ground-breaking Walking With Dinosaurs.

As you head up the fourth floor staircase, you're greeted by the head of Titanosaurus – a dinosaur too big to even completely fit in the room it's displayed in – and follow all the way through almost two hundred million years of history, from Coelophysis to Tyrannosaurus Rex.

We've travelled the world in two museums today, been witness to evolution and revolution, but as it's time to head up Broadway to the Beacon Theatre, our history lesson is not over yet.

Doug Lancio teases and twists the neck of his guitar, drawing a shimmering, disorienting sustained note. The music sitting underneath Dylan wouldn't be out of place on a Nick Cave record. Dylan is singing – carefully, clearly, passionately – to the Black Rider. Matching the guitar work from Lancio, Dylan's voice glides up and down over the notes of each final line in the verses.

It's this clarity of singing that lets the audience really get involved with the content of the lyrics; gone are the days of not knowing what songs have been played until a fellow member of the crowd informs you that Like a Rolling Stone has been and gone, and get involved they do; there are ripples of laughter around us as Dylan warns the Black Rider to leave his wife alone and go home to his own while the whole room gets a kick out of Dylan's juvenile Juvenal joke later in the song.

Despite the laughter from the crowd, the music is eerie. It's spare but what is being played is being played with a threat and that fits the song as multiple lyrics continue Dylan's latter day penchant for threatening violence against anyone who does him wrong.

Straight from threats to reassurance, after Black Rider the band lock into a toetapping groove that has us dancing in our seats as soon as it starts. Dylan comes in with the lyrics to I'll Be Your Baby Tonight. He sounds urgent as he sings, firing the lines out quickly but with precision. He drifts in and out of the original melody but what's most enjoyable is when he locks into a new rhythm and melody with his vocal line and rapidly builds the words up before releasing the line with a sustained note at the end. It's outrageous that sixty years into his career, Dylan is arguably doing his best singing now.

The song descends into an instrumental break where Dylan and the guitarists trade solos – I'm no longer missing Charlie Sexton now, all the musical spaces are being filled. Dylan's piano is jazz inflected and the guitars sound like they're from a garage rock band. There is no reason for this to work but it absolutely does, I'm lost in the swell of it all and then the band modulates up into the song's coda, Dylan reassures us one last time that he'll be our baby tonight and it's all over.

Up next is the stalking, meandering My Own Version of You. This word-heavy song has the attention of everyone in the room the whole way through, Dylan is reading from a lyric sheet but the fans in the room are keeping up with every allusion, reference and quote and laughing or applauding in all the right places.

Dylan is down in the groove, too, and enjoying himself on this one. A few cries ring out in the audience at the end of the sixth verse and Dylan looks up from his piano into the room with a smile across his lips. "Sure", escapes from his mouth, sustained a while and in time with the music and sends up a more raucous appreciation from around the room. At the end of the next verse, Dylan trails away from the last line with an "aw, yeah" that is reminiscent of Phil Harris' trademark exhalations of joy when singing (whether on The Dean Martin Show or as Baloo the Bear in Jungle Book).

"I can see the history of the whole human race" Dylan sings, and he lets us get a glimpse of a fair portion, as well, by name checking Al Pacino, Marlon Brando, Leon Russell, Liberace, St John the Apostle, Freud and 'Mr Marx' (Karl, presumably, not Groucho), by referencing work by

Shakespeare, Billie Holiday, Sinatra, Mary Shelley and singing about wars and crusades throughout human history.

Early Roman Kings, up next, could be about the history of the whole human race, too. No longer driven along by that Muddy Waters Mannish Boy riff, the song still packs a punch.

Between Early Roman Kings and To Be Alone With You, Donnie Herron picks up his violin and takes us back a couple hundred years with a gorgeous fiddle line, back to the American frontier again. Dylan is in frontier mood, too; singing about being together under the moon and under a star spangled sky.

The song is packed with new lyrics, the ones used on Shadow Kingdom, and things turn ugly when Dylan switches from flattery to threatening in order to get his love alone. In one verse, he'll hound her to death and in the next (either side of an extended piano solo and bridge) he's wryly feigning ignorance of a murder committed at his own hand. To really hide the horror of his actions, these lines are sung with some of his sweetest vocals of the night so far and ramp us up into the finale of the song. Tom Waits once said "I like beautiful melodies telling me terrible things", and it's hard to recall a finer combination of those two components than this.

Earlier the threatening Black Rider swept into the reassuring I'll Be Your Baby Tonight. Here, on To Be Alone With You it's like Dylan has mixed the two up in a tank and pulled out the new lyrics.

After the song has finished Tony Garnier moves to his double bass, Donnie Herron moves to accordion and Dylan shuffles the papers atop his piano before planting his hands square on his keys. Key West (Philosopher Pirate) rolls into the room; from the stage, of course, but it also seeps in through the walls and up from the floor. It's in the air. It drifts through the ears and minds of everyone in the room and pushes every other thought out of our heads. While Key West is playing no other songs exist but this one.

Bob Britt's guitar cascades behind Dylan, rising before the chorus and allowing Dylan to climb that ascent to put his power into the next six lines. Britt plays a lick to signal the end of the chorus and Dylan expertly echoes the phrase on his piano.

With each verse the imagery is piled up, the picture becomes clearer but still just out of focus and out of sight as if the radio signal we're picking this song up on is never quite strong enough. When Dylan pushes all his energy into lines like "feel the sunlight on your skin", you do feel a warmth rippling over you. With the delivery of "the healing virtues of the wind" you really do feel the breeze blowing through you.

The man next to me is sobbing, my eyes are full of tears and my partner beside me is crying, too. It's impossible not to be moved by this song, by this performance. The ten minutes it takes for Dylan to take us to Key West pass by in an instant and they last forever.

Dylan doesn't give us any time to catch our breath or gather our emotions as his band have already ramped into a rocking Gotta Serve Somebody. Charley Drayton is really whipping the band along from behind his drums, the urgent shuffle beat like a runaway train.

The guitars of Bob Britt and Doug Lancio are unchained now and they are frenetic as they rock and roll their way through the track. Dylan is clearly enjoying the chaos with a series of sustained "aww"'s and "oh yeah"'s both in the choruses and instrumental breaks. Every head in front of us is bobbing and bouncing, we are dancing in our seats; you can't help but be moved by this energetic rhythm. All night long the band have been a level above Friday night's show and it's most telling here where the guitarists are unshackled and Dylan's unbridled joy is evident in response.

When finally the audience has quietened down at the end of the song – the rough and rowdy applause goes on for some time at the close of every number – a voice cuts through the room; a voice that isn't Dylan's. "Pretty boy Floyd!" is shouted from somewhere in the crowd. Dylan smirks and looks out into the room "I'll tell you, you've come to the wrong place" he says into the microphone through a laugh. "They got Springsteen on Broadway, maybe then. You got the wrong show!". On stage, the band crack up and so do all of the audience.

(Incidentally, though Springsteen has recorded Pretty Boy Floyd more recently than Dylan has, it seems Dylan has performed it live in concert more times – twice to Springsteen's once. It is also one of the seventy five songs namechecked or referenced in Murder Most Foul).

While the crowd laugh and joke about Dylan's remark the band ready their instruments and kick into the gorgeous opening to I've Made Up My Mind to Give Myself to You. The music seems to be based loosely upon Jacques Offenbach's barcarolle "Belle nuit, ô nuit d'amour" (as examined by Laura Tenschert in the excellent collection of essays Dylan at 80: It Used to Go Like That and Now It Goes Like This).

Dylan's voice is so smooth, so full of life and experience and so tender that from the second he starts singing this song you are overwhelmed with emotion. By the time he gets to the end of the first verse and drags out a note impossibly long, using up every last breath and emotional memory he has to fill the words up with such meaning, you have given yourself up to the song.

Whether he has made up his mind to give himself to his love, his muse or his audience, it doesn't matter. It's the most honest I've ever heard him. Sam Cooke once asserted that "voices ought not to be measured by how pretty they are. Instead they matter only if they convince you that they are telling the truth". Here, singing this song, Dylan has convinced us that whoever he is singing to or about, he is telling the truth, and he's telling it in his prettiest possible voice.

He takes a piano solo, his most economic playing of the night, that wouldn't be out of place in any classical piece. No wasted notes, no flamboyant fills, just every note that needed to be played.

We're both crying again, silently and openly. This song is overwhelmingly beautiful, heartfelt. It is about as perfect a song as he's ever written. I turn to my right, to the woman I'm here with, as Dylan sings that he'll go "far away from home with her" and I think about the three and a half thousand miles that we've travelled together to be here tonight.

This song would have been worth travelling that distance by itself; it would have been worth the cost of flights and hotels and taxis and tickets combined just to hear this perfect piece of music so perfectly performed.

Ever the trickster, putting Melancholy Mood next in the setlist wrongfoots me and most likely a lot of the audience. I loved the Sinatra years at the time and all of those songs, but it's hard to focus on Melancholy Mood with the weight of I've Made Up My Mind To Give Myself to You hanging over it.

As quickly as it comes, it's gone again and Dylan is back behind his piano for another Rough and Rowdy Ways heavyweight.

Mother of Muses is a religious song on the record, and in the room it is a religious experience. Dylan revealed to us the creative process earlier on with My Own Version of You but now he's revealing the creative spirit to us with his prayer that the Mother of Muses, Mnemosyne, sing for him. In this hall, with this artist singing these words in this voice, we have gone beyond the concert experience.

Dylan has always been an important artist to his fans, he's always had a huge cultural impact, but in the second half of his career he has cemented his place in history; alongside Homer, Virgil, Dante, Shakespeare, Milton and Keats and it's by writing songs like these that have done that. Perhaps these works, Dylan's work from "Love and Theft" onwards will eventually last through time longer than even his groundbreaking early records.

Mother of Muses tonight stops you in your tracks, you hang on every word and it doesn't feel like it's being sung to us as much as through us. It almost doesn't feel like it's being sung by a voice, at all, as much as it is sung by a power. It feels ancient and of the earth, of the world and is simply channelling through Dylan.

It calls for a standing ovation at songs end and everyone stays on their feet as the band crash into Goodbye Jimmy

Reed. The volume has cranked up and Dylan is back to boogieing behind his piano. How easily he slips between his characters on stage.

In the audience we're painting the town, I'm swinging my partner around and we don't stop moving the entire time. Nowhere else will you be moved to tears in one song and moved to dance like this the next as you will in the room with your favourite artist, especially having been denied the experience for so long through the pandemic.

Goodbye Jimmy Reed is great fun, and a great way to close the show. He's saying goodbye to every one of us, too, and to the songs he's left behind for us.

At this point on Friday night Dylan thanked the audience, introduced his band ("Charley is some drummer, oh boy!") before telling us "it's awful nice to be back in the Big Apple. We saw Broadway; the Statue of Liberty, Wall Street, Times Square, all of it, Empire State Building, 5th Avenue. I'm glad to see it's coming back alive". Considering his connection to the city, Dylan himself could be listed as a landmark to see here.

Tonight during the thank-you's, instead of listing places, Dylan references the people who have lived here. "Why, thank you everybody. I want to thank you on behalf of my band as well. It's good to be back here in the Big Apple. I know George Gershwin lived here. Jackie O. Herman Melville was born here. But we're talking about the greats? Sylvester Stallone is also from here."

I've not been to many gigs before where the artist could draw a consecutive round of applause for Gershwin (whose 1927 composition "Soon" Dylan expertly performed at a

Gala in Brooklyn in 1987), Onassis, Melville (whose novel Moby Dick Dylan cited as one of three major influences in his Nobel Speech, alongside All Quiet on the Western Front by Erich Maria Remarque and Homer's Odyssey) and Stallone.

Dylan continues "If you haven't seen his latest movie, you've got to go see it. It's called…" he turns to his band, laughs and then back at the mic, "what's it called?". It's reminiscent of his 1991 Grammy Lifetime Achievement acceptance speech. "Oh yeah, it's called Last Something. Last Blood! That's right. Last Blood. I tell you, it should have won an Academy Award, but of course it didn't. Maybe next time."

With this, he moves into the band intros. "Talking about greatness, there's Charley Drayton playing on the drums. Doug Lancio is on guitar. Bob Britt is playing one of the guitars." He pauses to let the crowd show their appreciation but cuts Britt's cheer short by asking him "Bob, show them all you can play that guitar behind your head, or just put it back even if you don't play it!" Britt duly does and runs the guitar around behind him to Dylan's obvious delight, "there you go!", he lets out a laugh and his smile lasts all through the rest of the introductions, "Donnie Herron's playing steel-guitar. Donnie's from Fort Smith, Arkansas. One of the occult centres of the world", which would explain Donnie Herron's mystical ability on so many instruments, "and I uh, well I can't tell you how great this guy is, he's been great for a long time, Tony Garnier".

Without missing a beat, the band sweep into Every Grain of Sand. In the audience we've stayed on our feet. This song feels special when you hear it on 1981's underrated

Shot of Love album, but even more so in person. It's one of Dylan's songs that sounds like it's always playing; when it's on you can't remember a time when you weren't hearing this song and can't remember a time these words weren't working their way into your brain and coursing through your veins.

Dylan speaks to the human condition and Every Grain of Sand may be the first time he tapped into it in such a profound way; not just speaking of love and death, living and moving, but singing about everything it means to be human, to be alive all at once. When he wrote it he was just about to turn forty.

He's now singing it forty years on, with all the experiences he's lived through since evident in his voice, all the longing and loving, all the caring and hurting, all the travelling, believing and creating he has done since. When he sings about hearing the ancient footsteps and the motion of the sea, we hear it too. When he tells us about broken mirrors, innocence, forgotten faces and trembling leaves, the masters hand and sparrows falling, we see and feel all of it, too.

At the end of the song the band line up across the stage and look out over the adoring audience. The level of appreciation for this man is showing in the room; everyone is on their feet, everyone is clapping, screaming or cheering. Everyone is grateful to be here.

Despite what he sang in the final song tonight – sometimes I turn there's someone there, other times it's only me – we will always be right behind him.

We don't know what's going to come next in Dylan's story, or our own as the pandemic seems to have picked up pace again. The Rough and Rowdy Ways Worldwide Tour is set to run for three more years but it may have to take some detours along the way. Over the last ten years, Dylan has somehow grown better and better each year. It is an improbable turn in a career full of improbable turns. If you get the chance to see him on the road, like his posters used to say, don't you dare miss it.

But if indeed the door has closed forever more, we can at least always be thankful that there ever was a door.

ACKNOWLEDGEMENTS

Thanks of course to my uncle for introducing me to Bob Dylan way back when; to my mother for taking me to see him for the first time and accompanying me to further concerts in Philadelphia, London and Paris and for never getting too annoyed when I'd play my records too loud at home or wail along with my guitar in an effort to learn as many Dylan songs as I could, and for all her help with this book; it would not be the same as it is without her contribution. Thanks as well to the rest of my family, too – to my aunt, her husband and their two boys, to my nan and to my grandad – for tolerating my obsession and always for everything else, too.

Thank you to Emily for giving me the belief that I had it in me to put my experiences on paper and for inspiring me every day with her own creativity and her warmth.

Thanks to Jake for all the help and to the rest of the wonderful Bob Dylan community, both on and offline

– to Diane Williams and Laura Tenschert – who creates *the* premier Dylan podcast alongside Robert Chaney, Definitely Dylan – to Hollis Brown and HarryHew, thanks to Andreu and Natalie and Vincent, too. Also to James A. Craine, who's blog AsNaturalAsRain is a must to read and follow; and to Mark, Thomas, Emma, James, Anne-Marie, Keith, Olly and Joe. Dag, Davie, Melanie, Tom, Ross, Lola and Rebecca. To Tim, Allison, Sir Beef, asphaltmieze and Thelma, Brittany and Kathleen; Connor, Pat, Duncan and Constantine; Timothy, Toshikazu, Ret and all the rest – for the friendship, enlightenment and passion and compassion through the years.

I'm grateful to my friend Gwyn for understanding I could no longer make it to see Jerry Seinfeld with him at the Hammersmith Apollo the second that Bob Dylan announced a gig in Hyde Park for the same day.

Thanks to Hannah, Jack, Meera, Joshua and all at Troubadour for all the help and for helping me get this project off the ground and to everyone else in the business for their work in putting it together.

Finally, thanks of course, to Bob Dylan and His Band. Thanks for everything so far and all the rest to come. I'll see you back out on the road.

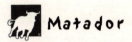 Matador

For exclusive discounts on Matador titles,
sign up to our occasional newsletter at
troubador.co.uk/bookshop